The Things I Wish I'd Said

Michele VanOrt Cozzens

McKenna Publishing Group
Indian Wells, California

The Things I Wish I'd Said

ISBN: 1-932172-21-1
LCCN: 2004108846

Cover Design by Leslie Parker

First Edition
10 9 8 7 6 5 4 3 2 1

Printed in the United States of America

Table of Contents

For My Daughters

The Things I'm Saying Now

I know it's happened to you. I know because I've yet to find anyone who cannot relate to this, and I've asked about fifty people. So, considering there are only nine personality types out there, you're bound to relate. Here's what I mean:

You find yourself in a situation that takes you by surprise. A confrontation, perhaps, and you're expected to respond. You say what immediately comes to mind—something simple, maybe even inane—and walk away. Seconds later the perfect comeback line pops into your brain and you wish in vain for the opportunity to push an imaginary rewind button to recite the enlightened script inside your head.

It happened just yesterday while I sat on the cold, concrete floor of our garage preparing six hundred cake boxes for the local elementary school's fall festival. It was just one more Hell Week project to ensure my full initiation in the under appreciated sorority for stay-at-home-moms called volunteerism. I was asked to sort the cake boxes because I'm still a stupid freshman in the school of volunteerism and said yes only because I like the chairperson of the event. She told me it was "easy."

Easy? I should have noticed that sadistic glint in her eye before I drove to her house to collect the boxes from the forklift pallet. Perhaps "simple-minded" would more accurately describe this project, which took hours and provided brutal paper cuts to boot. (Have you ever lifted forty or fifty flat, cardboard cake boxes at once?)

Anyway, while I was in the midst of grumbling about the large sizes of the fourth grade classes, the phone rang. And on the other end was some-one with yet another request for my time. "We'd like you to teach Sunday school to our teenagers," said the caller, the children's minister at our Epis-copal Church. "You'd be GREAT at it!" She had a little too much zest in her tone and it had the same affect as sprinkling salt into my bleeding paper cut wounds.

Teaching Sunday school, hmmm. My first thought: *God, no!* There's no way I'd be great at teaching teenagers anything. And Sunday school takes teachers away from the service, which is one opportunity I have during my volunteer-packed weeks to do something for myself by listening to our rector's enlightening sermons. That and because of a few too many rebel-lious years as a product of parochial school (read Catholic) education, I felt I wasn't the best role model in this particular area. These teenagers would no doubt know far more about the Bible than I.

As she rambled on, outlining the curriculum designed to teach high school kids about the nine personality types based on the Enneagram (pronounced any-o-gram)—this is how I know that at least according to this theory, there are nine different personality types—I stopped listening and started formu-lating my response. I had already turned down her request to teach last year—citing my overextended volunteer efforts—and as a result, endured six months of self-inflicted guilt for my refusal. (It just goes to show, you can take the girl out of the Catholic church, but you can't take the Catholic church out of the girl.)

What I said—as my husband shot me *you're insane and if you take on any more volunteer work I'll kill you* looks—was : "I'll give it a try."

What I wish I'd said: "NO!" A plain and simple, Nancy Reagan NO.

If life were a TV sitcom, we'd all have scripts to provide us with ideal dialog for each situation around the bend. And we'd be funny. We'd also have personal trainers and hair and make-up people to help make us look good while reciting our funny lines.

But alas, life is no sitcom. And on the morning after a confrontation, I appear as attractive as a sink full of dirty dishes because I stayed awake most of the night devising the "should-a, could-a, would-a said" scenarios on the movie screen inside my head.

According to the Enneagram this trait qualifies me as a "Perfectionist." And yet after further research, I discovered I share as many personality traits with the Giver, the Performer, the Romantic, the Questioner, and the Protector.

That's five out of nine types, and having multiple personalities was another reason I probably wasn't a good choice for Sunday school teacher.

More importantly, however, I wondered how I could teach something carrying little meaning or credibility for me. I might just as easily teach the kids to judge their personalities by reading their horoscopes. After all, even the Bible mentions the constellations of the Zodiac (2 Kings 23:5), which is more than I can say for the Enneagram.

Like the Zodiac, the origins of the Enneagram go far back into history—maybe as far back as the initial Sufi secret societies in the Middle East. Introduced in the United States in the 1960s, the Enneagram—in Greek meaning, "nine points," is used today not only in religious education but in relationship counseling and recovery programs, and in corporate team building exercises. This theory proclaims we use our natural talents to develop our personalities in the first years of life as we learn to cope with other personalities outside the womb.

In other words, it's another way to point fingers at our parents for making us who we are.

I believe my own mother went through life as an "Observer," which is one who thinks rather than says things like, "help me avoid intrusions on my privacy and if I seem aloof, distant or arrogant, it may be that I am feeling uncomfortable." She was terribly, and I mean *terribly* shy. She had a gorgeous smile, but would sooner cover her mouth than laugh out loud and potentially expose anything internal.

My mother once told me a story about loaning a beautiful antique cradle to a friend, who had the surprise of her life when she found herself pregnant at the age of forty-eight. Since my youngest sister showed up just prior to her forty-third birthday, Mom knew the dreadful feeling of coming home from the doctor's office and breaking the news to an equally advanced-age daddy, who was counting the days until retirement. A kind and generous woman, my mother was just trying to help. And her friend, who loved antiques, happily accepted the use of this wooden cradle, a cradle that had been in my mother's family for generations.

Years later, when her friend's healthy baby girl had grown out of cradle stage and my mother's eldest daughter was about to be married, she asked her to return the cradle so that her future grandchildren could use it.

"That old thing?" replied the friend. "Oh, it was destroyed some time ago."

"Destroyed?" asked my mother (no doubt covering her mouth in horror).

"Yes, destroyed. It was stored out in the barn and something must have fallen on top of it and it broke into pieces. It was beyond repair."

Even though my mother didn't believe this story, she turned and walked away. It simply wasn't in her nature to question or confront.

I remember her recounting this tale to another friend—her best friend in fact—and each believed the story was made up. "Knowing how much she covets and respects antiques there's no way she would have stored this exquisite piece in a barn or have it in harm's way," said Mom.

"You know what you *should* have said?" suggested her friend. "You should have told her to gather the pieces and send them to you to see about having it repaired."

"I wish I had thought of that," lamented my mother.

If I had been in the same situation, I don't know what I would have done or said. Accusing an old friend of lying may destroy the friendship. And then again, if the so-called friend *is* lying, what kind of friend is she? It comes down to deciding what's more important, the antique or the old friend? For my mother, I think it was most important to stand back, not confront and move on. She never mentioned the cradle again.

My mother is no longer living, so I can't discuss the Enneagram theory with her and what we may or may not share in terms of personality or how her character traits affected my own. I do believe, however, that she, like myself, would have a long list of things she wished she'd said.

Don't we all?

Recently my husband returned from a painful and expensive dental procedure. It's called a deep cleaning and might be more accurately described as the dental hygienist's opportunity to administer not a kinder, gentler cleaning, but a crueler and more unusual punishment. For a while, every time we went to that dental office there was a different hygienist on staff. The dentist and his assistants along with an army of office workers remained consistent; however, they had a revolving door thing going on with the ones who treat you like naughty children if you've failed to floss fifteen times a day between visits. Meanwhile, this floss monkey informed my husband that in addition to the expensive deep cleaning procedure, he needed another crown—a piece of dental jewelry that might as well be the crown jewels for the price. Since we've already paid for thousands of dollars worth of dental work this year (who knew that middle age would require the refilling of all our childhood dental work?), he said he'd have to put it off for a while because of the expense.

"Well maybe if you got a winter job you could afford it," she said like the sassiest kid on the playground.

Now what kind of thing is that for a dental hygienist to say to a patient? It's one thing to scold patients for grinding their teeth or not using the "up comes the grass, down comes the rain, back-and-forth like a choo-choo train," approach to brushing, but we prefer to leave our budgetary matters to our financial advisor rather than our dental hygienist.

Since my husband and I own a seasonal business that we leave in the hands of a caretaker during the winter so we can spend time with our children (and volunteer our time in their school), I suppose she assumed we just sit around and don't floss our teeth in the winter.

When he told me what she had said, I immediately reached for the phone to report this very inappropriate remark to the office manager. His mouth was still numb, so he felt he couldn't make the call. But he stopped me. "I'll do it," he said. "Later."

The Things I Wish I'd Said

No doubt, later meant after he had developed the perfect script.

The perfect script may come as soon as you walk away from the scene or, as it often does for me, in the middle of the night. Take, for example, one night after I was on TV for a live, three-minute interview at a local news station. On the day of the interview, I paced around the house practicing out loud what I planned say about a book I wrote and a fund-raising effort my family was working on for herb awareness. The format allotted me three minutes to say everything I wanted to say about the book, the fund-raiser and the very heavy topic of the death of my niece—who died because she took a weight loss herb that caused her heart to fail.

Those had to be the fastest three minutes of my life. And did I say everything the way I had practiced or the way I wanted it to come out? I'm afraid not. So, there I was in the middle of the night replaying in my head the things I wished I'd said. Of course, I should have been sleeping, yet instead I obsessed over not only the way I could have used the time a little bit better, but also that my forehead, which happens to be as broad as a movie screen, appeared excessively shiny in the bright studio lights.

Note to self: Next time an interviewer asks for a brief synopsis, *give* a synopsis. And for pity's sake remember to use powder above the eyebrows!

Beginning in 1991, for two years I wrote a weekly column for a community newspaper in Oakland, California. The paper was *The Montclarion* and my column was "First Person Plural." Each week I wrote about life with my husband and friends in our urban forest community known as the East Bay in the beautiful San Francisco Bay area, where I lived for most of the 1980s and early 1990s. My writing requirements for this Lifestyle section column of 750-words, were that everything had to be "true and not too political." In other words, nothing too deep or too controversial. It was like peanut butter and Fluffernutter. Basic stream-of-consciousness stuff I made up in the shower, and then with a towel on my head, typed into my first generation Macintosh SE, which had a screen about the size of my hand.

During my stint as a columnist, I worked with approximately four different editors. Mainly there was one man who was the newspaper's copyeditor. He did a wonderful job. On the outside he seemed dry and cerebral—everything you'd imagine in a copyeditor—but he was a true stylist. He corrected my spelling and grammar and almost always understood my attempts to be funny. He rarely changed the meaning of my words or thrust of my message. (As opposed to another editor, for instance, who didn't know what a cicada was when I used it to describe the familiar summer buzz as background music to my piece. She insisted I call them "Midwestern cicada" since she hadn't heard them in the cities of New York or Oakland. I happen to know for a fact that cicada, a genus of homopteran insects known for the whirring noise made by the male are not exclusive to Midwestern landscapes.)

As I read through the columns I wrote over a decade ago, absorbing the younger opinions of all my former selves, there's plenty I could have said differently. Keeping in mind the day-older, year-wiser philosophy, I thought I might have much wiser things to express now that more than ten years have passed. I have, after all, grown up.

Am I older? Yes. But wiser? Hmmmm.

Frankly, this collection is just a lot about ME—the things I said then and the things I'm saying now. Please note that I do not consider my opinions brilliant or groundbreaking. So, if you're looking for that kind of thing, you've picked up the wrong book. This is simply a collection of stories and experiences— some funny, some serious—and I believe that many looking at the world from the tail end of the baby boom will relate to them.

It's entirely possible that this may also be a lot about YOU.

Meanwhile, back to me. Presently, I define myself as a wife and mother and admit that I regularly suffer from an acute case of mommy-brain. (Where did I set down my cup of coffee this time?) I hail from a middle class background and a Midwestern town and had the fabulous fortune of falling in love with a man who came from the other side of the tracks. (The side where the houses are bigger and the vacations are grander, and yet the work ethic remains strong.) I should point out that I didn't know this about my designated Mr. Right until one day when he picked me up at my temporary apartment in Oak Park, Illinois in a big, black Mercedes Benz and took me to dinner at the Chicago Yacht Club, where he was addressed as "Mr. Cozzens" and escorted to preferred parking. At this point I turned to him and asked, "*Who* are you really?" Since I was already madly in love with this beautiful, funny and hard-working man, who happened to be incredibly nice to me, I thought I hit one of life's little jackpots by becoming his wife. We've been together for nearly eighteen years, and as much as I talk about me, I happily go through my life as a *we*.

With the exception of the first column, "The War Hits Home," they're presented in no particular order other than a loose attempt at categories. Now that I arrange closets and drawer space for a household of people instead of just myself, I can't help but fixate on organization. Where my life was once full of it, today I feel like every other mommy I know who simply can't get enough of it. This piece about my sister Debra and her experience with the National Guard in what became known as Operation Desert Storm was the tryout piece I submitted to the editor who awarded me the job.

Along with other categories, I've grouped together several columns centered on our simple home life and the recurring theme of my Midwestern upbringing—a constant influence in my writing, my accent, and proof positive of something I am unable to change. I must note that while I provide the date the original column was published, the aftermaths have been written over a period of time. Throughout these passages I refer to my two children, sometimes by name, sometimes by age. So, I may refer to my baby, my preschooler or my seven year-old, perhaps suggesting that I am the mother of several more than two. Rest assured, I have only two children and will only have two, as we have made surgically sure of this fact. I also have one older brother and three sisters—two older, one younger—and each has tremendously influenced my life and consequently, my writing.

As this compilation has been a chance to review my past and expand upon some of my thoughts with perhaps, a more mature eye and a bit mushier brain, I believe that I (and maybe many) wouldn't change who I am today and what I said or did to find myself here. I have learned through this project that while you can't change the things that happened in the past—your experiences or the things you said—I believe, for what it's worth, you can revisit a previous thought and try again to get it right.

While my mom never went back and asked her friend for the pieces of her antique cradle, my husband *did* speak to the dental hygienist's office manager and I eventually told the Sunday school administrator that I only said yes to the teaching job so that I could look her in the face each Sunday. And I must admit that after the first time I was called to fill in, I loved being part of the teenager's Sunday school. As we sat in a classroom next to the church and discussed "Personality Type Five, The Observer," I thought of my mother and thanked God for working in mysterious ways, and especially for enabling me to cross paths with a delightful and intelligent group of young people. Realizing they had their entire adult lives ahead of them, I believed they were on the path to getting it right.

Regardless of this positive experience, I now intend to utter a plain and simple "no" to all further requests for volunteerism during the remainder of the school year. But first I have to finish the season coaching our undefeated soccer team, get through the next fund-raiser for the Educational Enrichment Foundation, which includes sorting through nine-hundred artwork submissions for a tee-shirt contest and attending weekly coffee clutch sessions at Le Buzz—Tucson's Northeast side's volunteer sorority hangout—and prepare a salad for sixty for our second grader's class party. And these are just the things I can think of right now.

Oh, how I wish I'd said, "no."

Chapter 1
Home Life

"May the gods grant you all things which

your heart desires, and may they give you a husband and

a home and gracious concord, for there is nothing

greater and better than this."

—Homer, *The Iliad*

The War Hits Home

February 22, 1991

The green light blinked with an easy steadiness indicating only one message on our answering machine. Usually when I enter the house with my husband, we listen to the recordings together. But this time I listened alone.

"It's your mother," said the oh so familiar voice—a voice that reminds me of telephone operator recordings saying things like, "If you'd like to make a call, please hang up and dial again."

"I'm sorry it always has to be your mother who tells you the bad news," she continued as five disasters raced through my mind. I sat down and prepared myself. She paused, started to speak again and her voice cracked.

My mother was crying.

"What!?" I said aloud. "What's wrong?" Hearing my alarm, my husband entered the room, sat next to me and heard the recording of a throat clearing through long-distance static.

"You should call your sister Debra. She's been notified by the National Guard that her unit is mobilizing to Saudi Arabia."

I don't remember what the message said after that because I immediately hit the speed call button labeled "Debra." And yes, it was true. My thirty-seven year-old sister had just returned home from a gas mask fitting at the National Guard Armory. She had only one week to organize her life before mobilization.

My sister joined the National Guard seven years ago while in medical school. Facing the high costs of out-of-state tuition, the Guard offered financial aid for the minimal commitment of one weekend per month and a two-week active duty requirement each summer, enabling her to be all she could be. Seeing her in military uniform usually prompted jokes from the family as we barked orders and called her names like "Hawkeye." It never occurred to us that she would ever be called to war. It never occurred to Debra either. The recruitment officers didn't emphasize things like overseas combat.

"I thought I might treat the wounded if there was ever a riot in the city or something like that," she said. "Call me stupid but did my enlistment really mean I'd be sent to war?"

Her six-year commitment ended last January. At the time she was two months pregnant, expecting her first child. The Guard suggested she stay in on a month-to-month basis. Since she was pregnant, active duty would be waived and she would only be paid for the weekends that she showed up. A pretty loose arrangement that, especially in light of the crumbling Berlin Wall and Cold War era collapse, seemed agreeable.

Her daughter, our niece Kayla, was born in August only twenty-six days after, unbeknownst to Debra, the National Guard put a freeze on all resignations and transfers. Iraq had invaded Kuwait and as a result things like motherhood became no excuse for avoiding active duty in the United States military.

That weekend military officers were faced with thousands of excuses, hardship cases and a ten percent rise in conscientious objectors. Ranging from parents phoning and saying things like, "he's our only son," to a woman with a knee brace recovering from recent surgery trying to get out on a medical excuse, nearly everyone had a sob story.

"Wasn't he your only son when he enlisted?" asked the Guard. And to the woman with the bad knee: "We'll get somebody to carry your bags, ma'am."

An inner-city black woman, a single mother who joined the National Guard to supplement an insufficient income was told to "find a neighbor" to take care of her ten month-old child. The National Guard, now mobilizing as the Federal Army, was after numbers. They needed to fill a quota. Yet even when my sister's husband, also a physician with ROTC training, offered to go in her place, the Army said no. It would take too much time and paperwork, they said.

The woman with the knee brace left on the bus, as did the woman with the ten month-old child. Neither of them had the support of friends and family that my sister had who helped her through the long days at the armory, always looking for last-minute solutions to allow her to stay with Kayla—a baby who was forcefully weaned away from her mother's breasts. Not only was Debra not around to feed her daughter, stress caused her milk to run dry.

The night before she was to leave, Debra was granted an honorable discharge based on a very real case of postpartum depression. At the news our family celebrated and Debra stripped off her Army gear one item at a time, giving away future Halloween costumes to her nieces and nephews.

Now for those of you who may also have family members and friends who have honored their commitments and are presently in the Persian Gulf or preparing to go, please don't frown upon my sister. One look at this small, beautiful woman dressed in army fatigues, crying along with her three month-old infant as she battled to wean her from breast milk to bottle in too short a time, would be enough to change anyone's mind about who should and should not be sent to war.

Home is the Loser

My newspaper column had two criterion. "Material should be true and not too political." Looking back at my first column, the piece I submitted to get the job, I believe it is very political and, perhaps, the most political piece I published. Depending on your current views, it may even border on the politically incorrect. Keep in mind that in 1991 we had only begun to taste the new age of political correctness and I obviously sensed potential repercussions by asking readers not to "frown upon my sister."

The Things I Wish I'd Said

Several frowned. They saw her only as a privileged, caucasian woman. A doctor married to a doctor. They felt she didn't deserve the "preferential treatment" and should have served her country.

I wish I had stressed my point a bit stronger. I wanted them to see her as a mother.

Thirteen years later, from the perspective of a mother—one who happily and without interruption breastfed her children until they decided to stop—I stand behind my belief that active military duty is no place for pregnant women *or* nursing mothers. Our responsibility as mothers is first to our children—then our country. Our military and our government understands the need to protect the pregnant woman and the unborn fetus, but once that fetus becomes a baby and is still attached to its mother—depends on its mother for the healthiest nourishment it can receive—all "protections" are lifted.

Is it any surprise my sister suffered from postpartum depression?

When I was pregnant people gave up seats for me, opened doors and helped me carry groceries. Today I see signs in grocery store parking lots reading, "Reserved for Pregnant Women." Instead of a wheelchair illustration there's a stork. After the babies arrive, attitudes change. People stop giving up seats and parking places. Old ladies with painted red mouths stop you in the grocery store, stick their fingers in your face and tell you need to keep your baby from screaming in public. Business travelers sneer at you for spoiling their cross-country flight because your baby cries or your toddler kicks the back of their chairs.

Life is sacrosanct in the form of a pregnancy—but what about the sanctity of the babies?

Let me backtrack a bit. In 1991 war was a foreign notion. I believed wars only happened in history books, in my World War II vet dad's long-winded stories at the dinner table, and in other parts of the world. In school I learned that wars were caused by political, ethnic and religious animosities; but with the outbreak of the Gulf War, it became clear that wars were, are and will continue to be about natural resources. The issue of war may be coupled with or even disguised as political, ethical, ethnic and religious conflicts; however, all pipelines, roads and the SUVs that drive on them lead to oil.

On the day the Gulf War began my husband and I were as dazed and confused as we had been in high school while tuning out of reality and into Led Zeppelin. While some of our first memories centered on protests over American involvement in Viet Nam, we learned as children that war was just plain wrong.

I recall a neighborhood birthday party where a sixth grade girl named Liz danced with too much soul for a white girl to Edwin Starr's "War". Her smooth, dishwater blonde hair swung wildly as she moved to the rhythm and sang, *"War: What is it good for? Absolutely nothin!"* And I further recall this same girl, who seemed so much older and more sophisticated than the rest of us, announcing to our catechism class that Nixon ended the war in Viet Nam. "Isn't that terrific?" she said to a room full of oblivious adolescents wanting to be anyplace other than a Catholic school classroom on a Saturday morning. And with the end of this war, Viet Nam flattened into the history books as big mistake and a waste of far too many lives. One trip to the memorial in Washington D.C., where a black granite wall displays just over 58,000 names of those killed, brings the wrongness of it right into your soul.

So, how does one go from childhood lessons that something is wrong to supporting a government that tags the operation du jour with a catchy name, "Operation Desert Shield" and then, "Desert Storm?" Do we all run to Wal-Mart and buy flags to display outside our homes and buy our kid's red, white and blue tee-shirts?

Well, we didn't really do that until the horrendous acts of September 11, 2001, when hijacked airplanes slammed into American icons, and war truly hit home for all of us; however, by this time the concept of war had become much more familiar. And this is because of what happened when Iraq invaded Kuwait. It therefore wasn't as shocking when the United States' ensuing action in first Afghanistan and now Iraq, once again drew our servicemen and women away from home.

The Things I Wish I'd Said

• • •

Debra's call to active duty in the autumn of 1990 was unfathomable. And my heart-wrenching reaction wasn't simply because I didn't want my sister to be sent overseas. It was because only a few months earlier, I flew to Michigan to attend the ritual known as a baby shower for my "advanced age" sister, who had finally decided to have a child. I hadn't even met my new niece when I tried to comprehend why her mother faced a military order to put her baby on a bottle of formula and answer to her government—to a cause bigger than her own.

Mother's milk paled in comparison to the world's thirst for oil.

Women don't need to be sent to war in order to be victims of war. According to the organization Global Women's Strike, women and children are the majority of those killed and wounded in armed conflicts worldwide and make up eighty percent of refugees. As lifegivers, war is a direct conflict to the very nature of womanhood.

In the United States, after women stood beside their brothers and protested the Viet Nam war, they took off their bras and once again turned their protests against gender inequality, fighting for rights in the workplace, along with the right to choose. My sister chose to go to medical school, chose to enlist in the National Guard to help supplement her tuition and then chose to have a child. She was an equal to her physician husband with ROTC training, who offered to go to Saudi Arabia in her place. But there was one area where this man and this woman were not equals and that was in their ability to breastfeed their baby.

On the day my sister was called to war I wondered, in our fight to be recognized as equals, did we forget the importance of our differences?

The sad fact is that because of the stress, her breast milk dried up anyway. She'll never get the opportunity to go back and breastfeed her only child. What a loss.

I know a man in Tucson who was called to active duty in the National Guard shortly after September 11, 2001 requiring the abandonment of his wife and two young children for at least two years. His orders were extended. He's still away. As his young children will only be this age now, he won't get the chance to go back and see his son's spelling bee victory or the expression on his daughter's face the day she received a perfect score in the skating competition. In a military town like Tucson, the home to Davis Monthan Air Force Base, and in towns across the country, his is just one of many stories of National Guardsmen leaving home to honor their commitments.

As the current conflict rages on in the Middle East, each time I see a sign in someone's front yard reading "Support our Troops," or see yellow ribbons tied around old palm trees, my heart goes out to our soldiers overseas, and even more to the families inside the homes they've left behind.

Because anyway you look at it, when war hits home, home is the loser.

The King is Definitely Dead

March 8, 1991

"Bad news. Elvis really is dead. I saw his grave and everything."

These were the only words I could think of to write on the Graceland postcard I sent from Memphis to the man who is now my husband. You see, in this age of true confessions, I suppose it's time to admit that I am married to an Elvis fanatic.

Now, don't get me wrong. He's not the kind of guy who reports Elvis sightings at the local Burger King or dresses up in rhinestone-clad pastel costumes with big belts. He doesn't attend Elvis impersonator concerts (regularly, anyway), nor does he make annual pilgrimages to Graceland. He, in fact, has never been to Graceland.

I'm not sure how it all started, but my husband is known among our friends and acquaintances across the country as someone who craves collectibles of "the King." We've got more Elvis paraphernalia than we have room to display—or store. Ranging from designer plates from the Bradford Exchange to photo stills from his movies (the one with Ann-Margaret from *Viva Las Vegas* is a particular favorite), from Frisbees to Elvis earrings, picture disc LPs and a fresh-smelling bottle of Elvis shampoo, all this junk is displayed in one corner of our house and dedicated to Elvis Presley.

Since we moved to the Montclair hills and I became responsible for house decor, the wall-of-fame—as it's called—has shrunk a bit, sized down from the original. A few of those famous Elvis sneers can now be found in our—excuse me—my husband's garage. Walk by our house any time the garage door is open and you might think it's the "Elvis for City Council" campaign headquarters.

Although the first song we danced to at our wedding was "I Can't Help Falling In Love With You," our stereo only rarely plays Elvis recordings. But for me the sweet sound of Elvis' voice is the best part of the Elvis collection in this house. Singing talent was one thing crass commercialization and overexposure couldn't take away from the King of Rock and Roll.

As I mentioned, my husband has never been to Graceland, but I have the feeling that if he ever takes the seven-dollar house tour and pays the additional dollar for the tour of the now stationary touring bus or the $3.85 tour of the grounded private plane "The Lisa Marie," he might question his ambitious collecting. (My visit to Graceland was back in 1986 so tour prices may be even higher now.)

As I recall the only two words passing through my mind upon entering each room of the white-pillared, Southern mansion were "tacky" and "gaudy." The decor was as overdone as the movie plots in the films in which Elvis starred.

The friend I was visiting in Memphis, who took me to Graceland under protest, hadn't yet subjected himself to the tour and swore he never would. Yet since I convinced him I only wanted to do it to get souvenirs for the wall-of-fame, he conceded and joined me in an afternoon giggle fest. He snapped pictures of me in front of the pink-and-black Cadillacs, the motorcycle collection and next to the two-foot high stack of letters sent by fans to the U.S. government protesting Elvis' induction into the Army.

We laughed and gagged our way through the mansion from the back of the flock. Seeing the other visitor's backs and not their serious expressions, I assumed most people thought Graceland an amusing novelty.

I was wrong.

Behind the graffiti-covered, fortress-like walls and inside the musical-note-clad iron gates, Graceland stands as a shrine to fans of the late, great Elvis Presley. My friend and I were frowned at blatantly with "don't be cruel" expressions from worshippers due to our lack of respect.

Because my first reaction to the infamous "jungle room" decor was to open my mouth and say the word "yuck," I thought I would be ushered out by an angry mob. (What a curse it was on poor Elvis to have his sense of style stuck in the 1970s!)

I watched tears flow at his gravesite and listened with horror as the guide told us that his grave had to be moved from a public cemetery to the Graceland property because of all the vandalism.

At this, the last leg of the tour, I admit I experienced a sense of loss and definite sadness. Yet I couldn't figure out whether I felt more sorry for Elvis or for his fans. These days I am mostly sorry each time a friend finds the perfect housewarming gift for our wall-of-fame.

Just like Elvis ran out of time, we have run out of room.

Long Live The King

The column about the ultra famous Elvis Presley was responsible for getting me recognized for the first time. It was my first taste of Andy Worhol's fifteen minutes, and it happened in my own garage on the day I hosted a tag sale for a recently divorced coworker.

The garage of our Oakland, California abode, which looked out to a fairly busy thoroughfare, rivaled any Elvis museum. And while none of the Elvis paraphernalia was for sale, nearly everyone who stepped from the main sale area of the driveway inside the garage made offers on everything from the giant, tri-colored Elvis tapestry to the Elvis Frisbee disc.

One man came in, looked around and noticeably darted his eyes back-and-forth from Elvis' face to mine. "You're that columnist," he said like a sleuth who had just solved a puzzling case.

"Wow," I said. "People actually read my column?"

At the time of the tag sale, I had published several columns and let readers know not only about my Elvis-collecting husband, but also about one of our other quirks, which was the sport of disc golf and the Frisbee collection that coexisted with Elvis paraphernalia. Between these two collections screaming from the rafters and the grainy black-and-white image of my face smiling ear-to-ear at the top of each column, I credited the man who recognized me as a fairly good detective. "I never miss your work," he said. "Are you going to keep going on this, get syndicated and then turn them into a book?"

As for the Elvis collection, most of it is packed up and stored in the same boxes we used to move away from California in 1993. Although the fervor of Elvis gift-giving has subsided, many who know the man in my life still can't resist sending him Elvis ornaments at Christmas or Elvis pictured on birthday cards. Like the world of Elvis impersonators, it's like an old joke that just won't go away.

Here's what I wish I'd said: Stop sending us all the Elvis crap!

I returned to Graceland in 1996 and pushed around my daughter in a stroller on the grounds and carried her on my hip throughout the house while my husband experienced the tour for the first time. In ten years nothing had changed. At least not at Graceland.

I, on the other hand, had evolved from a single girl on the road into a wife and mother. And rather than bunk with a friend in Memphis, during our visit we stayed at the splendid Peabody Hotel. I told my husband I wanted to stay there for our toddler to witness the famous parade of ducks that waddle through the luxurious lobby each afternoon. But the truth was, *I* wanted to see those silly ducks and I wanted to feel sophisticated by telling people that's where we stayed. In retrospect, however, I felt that spending close to four-hundred bucks on the room was a waste of money. A visit to Graceland, however, is anything but a waste of money. And the second time I went there, perhaps following my husband's lead, I was much more respectful.

Elvis was a phenomenal talent and gave to the world everything he had, paying the ultimate price of super-stardom.

The fascination with Elvis Presley remains strong throughout the world. (It has been reported that he continues to make upwards of $40 million each year from the grave.) Even more amazing is the Virginia-based Vaughan-Bassett Furniture Company's line of Elvis furniture that includes a "Love

Me Tender" bed and "Burning Love" heart-shaped mirror. Doug Bassett, the company's vice president of sales and marketing and great-grandson of its founder said he came up with the idea for the Elvis line while stranded in Memphis during Elvis week one summer and brokered a deal with Elvis Presley Enterprises. Now that's a visionary! When *I* visited Graceland I merely felt sorry for Elvis for having left that mansion full of tacky furniture as his legacy. But this guy Bassett hound-dogged a hunka-hunka burnin' profit as the first 3,000 bedroom sets sold out in gold record time.

While we don't intend to buy anything from the Elvis line, we still hold Elvis in high regard. Every Christmas we listen to his Christmas songs while decorating our tree and the kids hit the play button on our favorite Elvis ornament and sing along until we can't stand it. "I don't need a lot of presents to make my Christmas bright . . ." (The funny thing is, our kids DO need a lot of presents to make their Christmas bright.) Hanging from a suction cup on our kitchen window is a springy, six-inch Elvis-in-a-white-jumpsuit sculpture, presented by an old friend who visited last Thanksgiving. This year that same friend plans to come for Christmas. And I won't be the least bit surprised if he brings along a "Blue Suede Shoe Rack" wrapped with a big, red bow.

The king may be dead, but the joke will never die.

Just Saying No

June 4, 1991

Starting at 6:00 p.m. nearly every weeknight, it happens. It's as predictable as the morning alarm, as insistent as a whistling teakettle and more annoying than screeching nails on a chalkboard. The ghost of Alexander Graham Bell dances a jig in our living room. Yes, our phone starts ringing like it's telephone happy hour. Yet there's nothing about these phone calls that make us smile.

These aren't friends calling, mind you. Friends know better than to call during possible dinner hours. These are people who address us as Mr. or Mrs. and always pronounce my husband's last name incorrectly.

This is the key that activates my hostility button. His name does not have a long o. Our friends know this. People trying to sell us aluminum siding, blacktop or magazine subscriptions do not. Nor do those seeking political or charitable contributions.

Almost like an electronic answering machine (which I immediately lament not having let pick up the call) I respond to the mispronunciation by saying, "There's no one here by that name." Then I hang up.

It's called guilt-free rejection. It's an easy way to just say no to the pusher by never giving him the opportunity to ask.

What is it with these people anyway? Where did they learn that interrupting people during their first quiet hours at home with a well-practiced sales pitch for time-share property in Tahoe was a good tactic?

The Things I Wish I'd Said

These phone calls have gotten so bothersome that we're considering an unlisted phone number. But I resent being forced into this action. Aside from missing the initial thrill of getting the new phone book and finding your name, there's always the possibility of making yourself inaccessible to the people from whom you really do want to receive calls.

Can't the phone company put an asterisk by the names of those who will verbally abuse anyone who calls at dinnertime with a sales pitch?

We've gotten rid of the doorbell ringers by taping up a tacky little note reading, "No solicitors of any kind, please." This seems to be doing the trick. But before I scare off everyone, I don't mind the occasional uniformed Brownie selling Girl Scout cookies who might knock on our door. Anyone who doesn't yet have the word "solicitor" in her vocabulary is still welcome.

Which brings us to the mailbox—yet another victim of modern marketing mania. Ever since our name went on record as tax-paying homeowners, we've received a rash of mail from proprietors who are, I guess, above going door to door. These are the accountants, lawyers, dentists and chiropractors who ask for our business by means of a "welcome to the neighborhood" letter.

Please note all you people who waste time, paper and postage, we refuse to open these letters on principle alone. It's our way of saying, "Don't call us. We'll call you."

And who is this guy who keeps throwing little plastic bags containing a pastel-colored note and a small rock onto our driveway? Picking up these baggies and throwing them away is even more annoying than raking and hauling eucalyptus leaves.

I realize that I'm responsible for the barrage of mail order catalogs that have been delivered of late due to my subscription to *Better Homes and Gardens* and a Spiegel Credit card. Since acquiring these things it's as if someone highlighted my name and address with a florescent flag screaming, "She's a buyer!" How many magazines do they think I want to read? And how much brick-a-brac do they think my modest little house can hold?

You know, I could have a collection of fifty-two Visa Gold cards if I had responded to every offer found in my mailbox. It would be like a full deck of credit cards. I could make up a new card game—"Fifty-two pick-up *and* delivery!"

At the suggestion of my sister, six months ago I wrote to this phantom organization in New York called "Mail Preference Service" hoping to get away from the zillions of mailing lists that have all my vital statistics. But they never responded. I guess they preferred not to read *my* letter.

It seems the only way out of this marketing mire is to continue to take the simplest advice whenever somebody tries to sell me something I don't want, and that is to "just say no."

LorenaBobbit.com

I'm happy to report that eleven years after I wrote this column, I hold a phone book in my lap that uses a large, black diamond after the names of customers who "prefer NOT to be contacted by telemarketing or direct mail organizations." We don't have that diamond by our phone numbers but we do have the new invention known as "caller I.D." Let it be known that while our telephone answering machine has found its way into the appliance graveyard, our state-of-the-art "Voice Mail" secretarial system certainly takes care of the numbers registering as "Unavailable."

Unavailable, ha! What this says to us is that the caller is simply a solicitor in unavailable clothing. There are other calls that come in on the screen as "Private," however, I have two or three friends who block the identification of their calls and when I see that word, it might as well say something like "Wendy, Bonnie or Anne" for as much privacy it affords them in our house.

The bigger issue these days is with the scum showing up in my email mailbox. It's called SPAM. I don't know how that term came about or whether or not it's a clever acronym, but the junk mail it identifies is certainly as inedible as the stuff in the can. I just completed a little experiment and checked my email for the first time today. It's Sunday. Easter Sunday to be more precise. So, I thought I might be spared from the explicit, pornographic garbage circulating on the World Wide Web. Nothing doing. I had thirty-four pieces of mail and only four were from people I know. That leaves twenty-nine messages trying to sell me anything from free porn and the opportunity to enlarge my penis to "Sexy Asians, Latinas, Ebonys and Americans," and business opportunities offering "Cash in a Flash." (Looking over my shoulder, my husband just asked if I was sure it didn't read, "cash in the flesh?")

America On Line offers an address to which SPAM can be reported, but each time I tried to dump something in that mailbox, I received a message saying it was full. (It was like the phantom Mail Preference Service scenario all over again.) I understand there are SPAM-free email services available and may look into switching over; however, it feels a bit too much like moving. And for as many times as I've moved over the years, I'm tired of sending out change-of-address notices. I've also heard about downloadable software, or shareware to keep your mailbox free of solicitations. But they either don't make a version for Macintosh or I haven't found it yet.

There must be a solution. If video killed the radio star and caller ID killed the phone solicitor, what will kill the messages that continually suggest I need to enlarge my penis?

Lorena Bobbit, where are you when we need you?

Home Improvement

November 19, 1991

Every time I finish a project at home, I grab my aching back and swear that next time I'll hire someone else to do it. Whether it's painting a room, sewing a curtain or laying a hardwood floor, I know there're plenty of professionals out there who could do a much better job than I. They advertise in this newspaper every week. They have licenses.

Professional contractors must know the secrets to avoiding lower back pain. And I'm sure they don't care if their fingernails are stained and chipped. I don't care about their backs and nails either. I just want the project completed quickly, professionally and . . . cheaply.

That's the problem.

I'm a home improvement cheapskate. And I've got the sore body and busted nails to prove it. It's hard for me to squeeze out $800 for a painter to finish our fourteen by fifteen-foot bedroom when I could do the job for the cost of the paint. And so what if I spill a few droplets of paint on the carpet? I can easily rationalize that I was planning to change the color of the rug anyway.

As for my sore neck and shoulders, well, the pain always goes away.

When we bought this fifty-year-old house it was in pretty good shape—structurally. But aesthetically? Help me. We're talking pea-pod green and egg-yolk yellow walls, along with moldy dirt brown carpeting covering a black linoleum tile floor.

The Things I Wish I'd Said

Enormous wooden room dividers split the living areas into small spaces making the place look like a doctor's office. They were the first things to go. And after tearing these structures from the walls, I had a lesson in how to spread that deliciously goopy white stuff called joint compound.

"Don't be afraid to use a lot," said my instructor/husband. "You'll sand off the excess later, before you paint."

I don't know why I thought painting was an easy job. It's among the hardest things I've ever done. Especially when I was perched high on an eight-foot ladder standing on top of the warning sign reading: "Do not stand on or above this step. You may lose your balance."

Since I had no other way of getting to the far reaches of the slanted, beamed ceiling, I pretended I didn't see that silly sign. It reminded me of the tags on pillows that read "Do not remove this tag."

Luckily, I didn't lose my balance.

Outside the house the flat lot (a real find in the Montclair hills) was covered almost entirely with ivy. Only the landscaper knew what was underneath all that growth. It took me two weeks of tugging, cutting, fighting and swearing at that stubborn ivy to find out.

But eventually I won that fight. And to my delight, the gardener before me had planted several rhododendron shrubs among other horticultural delights. Most of it survived the strangling of the ivy.

Gardening always puts a smile upon my face. I wouldn't even consider hiring somebody to do this job for me. In fact, every time I get a flyer in my mailbox or a business card stuck in my front door from some landscaper with a license, I'm offended. I feel like they've signaled out my yard as being something in need of a makeover.

Thank goodness the insides of our houses aren't exposed to interior designers who might be driving by.

My husband's buddy, Pete, is a carpenter by trade and has done about ninety percent of the work around our house. We don't pay him much. But we feed him. A fair trade, I suppose. With his experience, he acts as the foreman on every project and reduces my husband to the laborer position. "Get me the Phillips head!" he commands.

When Pete's around I act as the design director and critic. (Since the guy is literally color blind, my role is very important.) It has gotten to where every time I see him, I start visualizing another project. "Hey Pete," I say, "what would you think about knocking down this wall?"

He usually wiggles his mustache and says something like "no problem."

Last April just before my parents came to visit, I broke down and hired a real painter to do the spare bedroom—their room—and complimented myself for being so smart. The job was done quickly and cleanly.

Unfortunately that same painter's estimate for the job on our bedroom was more than double what we paid six months earlier. The recession is hitting everyone, I guess. As I type these words with paint-stained fingertips, I realize it's hitting me in the lower back.

Time to call Pete.

Home Improvers Anonymous

That California cottage, all thirteen hundred square feet of it, was a wonderful training ground for home improvement and construction projects. With the experience we garnered there in three short years, we naively believed that we had evolved into qualified carpenters.

Note: There's a reason why the licensed contractors you hire to tackle the job of turning your concepts of a dream home into a reality charge as much as they do. It's hard work and in order to do it properly, it takes a great deal of good old-fashioned know-how. In other words, training. When it comes to putting a roof over your head, you want to be sure it stays over your head.

But one thing I'd like to say about residential contractors, and I believe I've had enough experience with several different so-called professionals (in several different states) over the years to be qualified to make this comment, is that they may be fabulous at what they do with a hammer and saw, but as a rule, they're lousy businessmen. They look great in their Levi's and tool belts, and they know the proper lingo regarding codes, joists, and R-factors; however, most of the ones I've worked with get a D-minus in the communications department. There's simply no class in the school of carpentry that teaches these guys the equivalent of a bedside manner—or at the very least, how to return phone calls in a timely manner.

Here's a bit of advice I offer to anyone undergoing a home improvement or construction project: It takes twice as long as the contractor says, and costs twice as much. Most of them seem to believe it's wiser to tell you, the customer, what they *think* you want to hear instead of the truth. I for one, only want to hear exactly when they plan to get their workers off my property so I can wear my pajamas outside my bedroom during the wee morning hours instead of having construction-boot wearing, cigarette-smoking men with hammers lurking around my windows.

We sold our California home to buy a lot of Wisconsin dwellings in the form of a Northwoods resort. I mentioned in the column that our Montclair home was fifty-years old. The house and cabins we purchased some two thousand miles to the east were even older and showed no evidence of being built by professional carpenters. Floors slanted, roofs leaked and critters like red squirrels and bats lived in the walls. We lured the squirrels outside by hanging a birdfeeder, because as every Northern forest dweller knows, birdseed is the delicacy of the red squirrel world. And when hanging a bat house failed to lure away the flying mammals, we went through every bat eradicator listed in the yellow pages of three counties. They used methods from mothballs to one-way netting (where bats could get out but not get back in) and none could rid our old cabins of these irritating critters. As they scratched and flapped and partied all night during their after sunset mosquito feasts, they made it very clear that they had squatter's rights inside the rotting logs of these cedar cabins.

When we moved onto some real improvements, I was a happy carpenter on the you-build-it-from-scratch log-cabin kits we purchased to construct two nine hundred square foot dwellings. We built these to make our resort a year-round facility, and for me it was like playing with large scale Lincoln Logs.

After we cleared the designated areas, turning small trees into piles of next year's firewood, we called in professionals to dig and construct the foundations. Even if you don't know a thing about building a house, you can guess that any building won't be a building for long if it doesn't have a strong foundation. (At least we got that part right.) The crew stayed on until the shells were complete, and then it was time to dress these cabins like they were our newly birthed, naked children.

Having two buildings going up at the same time allowed us to make all our rookie mistakes on the first cabin. And we definitely made some mistakes. On the day we attempted to hang football field-sized sections of drywall on the ceiling, for example, it was like a group of ninety-eight pound weaklings trying to lift Mr. Universe-sized weights over their heads. We invited unsuspecting relatives up for a "weekend at the resort" and shamelessly strapped tool belts to their waists and put them to work. I think it was my white-collar-clad brother who came up with the brilliant idea to construct braces from two-by-fours to hold the drywall in place while someone screwed it into the ceiling beams. If any professional contractors had been around to witness our techniques, we would have been banned for life from any kind of carpenter's union.

But the cabins were completed and believe it or not, they're still standing.

One spring, we flew in our old pal Pete (remember Pete?) from California to help construct a new deck and screen-porch on one of the units. And it was just like old times at this old house. He and my husband, along with another friend, argued over who was the actual foreman on the project and ultimately, I settled the arguments (there was no question that at least in my mind, I was in charge) and shared in the project by slicing and dicing the window trim with expert skill on the chop saw.

The house we purchased in Tucson, designed to be our winter retreat away from the Snow Belt was only two or three years old. It wasn't exactly our dream house, but we had designs on it from the beginning. It had Santa Fe written all over it, with big open spaces requiring big furniture and I was happy to shop for it. It would have been easier had I not had a three-month-old infant and a two-year old in tow, but I managed. Furniture, especially oversized furniture can fill up spaces in a hurry. It was the discovery of every necessary utensil to make a kitchen an operating facility that drove me crazy. I made more trips to the local Target than anyone could make in a lifetime to purchase everything from a spatula to a paper towel dispenser, a dustpan to a baking pan.

I needed a bridal shower.

I thought my main focus during the first season would be furnishing and equipping the house; however, I had no idea that soon I'd become obsessed with turning our dusty, treeless backyard into an outdoor oasis. I blame my neighbor, Wilma Flinstone, for this. She has a beautiful back-yard—a true oasis. Mature, leafy trees shaded the area like a giant umbrella. A rock waterfall spouted refreshing cascades of cool water into a channel that meandered throughout the yard and into a pond. Small shrubs with bright fuscia flowers and electric pink bougainvillea punctuated the space inside a freeform concrete wall painted pink—a color she called Sonoran Sunset—and a small area just outside her covered patio was reserved for a patch of soft green grass. Grass in the desert? I never knew.

For the rest of our stint that season in the desert, we were under construction. We designated an area for the playground and went from there. And each fall when we returned to Arizona after six months at our Wisconsin resort, my eyes only saw projects.

Pandora's Box was officially open and I had a new mantra: "Hello, my name is Michele and I'm a home improvement junkie."

For years, we couldn't stop. We became so obsessed with home improvement that some of our friends started greeting us by asking, "what are you building now?" instead of saying hello. And while we did much of the work ourselves, for most projects we hired help. Once the kids came into our life, our priorities changed and it became a matter of valuing our time, ache-free appendages, and learning to no longer be cheap about it.

The good news is that our backs are no longer sore and our home is beautiful. But the bad news is, of course, that now we're broke.

My Foggy Garden

July 16, 1991

The fog is so heavy in the morning it pelts our home life a soft rain. It lures me to the windows, fills me with hope. Maybe, I think in my conservation mode, the garden will not need watering today.

The iris and rhododendron leaves glisten as though freshly bathed. The lilies—always taller—draw closer to blossom. The entire garden, still new and sparse, grows silently while the translucent puffs of cloud stroll past like neighbors walking their dogs.

The fog covers this Montclair hillside like a blanket pulled up tightly when the sun drops behind the tallest trees and the furthest mountain range, and it lasts through the morning. It closes us off, protects us from the rest of the world.

It makes me never want to leave home.

We rise early in this household. Well before the sun even thinks about burning off the fog. And in spite of the hour, everything buzzes with activity. The birds sing so loudly we hear them through closed doors and windows. They splash seeds from the feeders, forming a small carpet of food on the ground below—an easy meal for the clumsy, bloated mourning doves. Squirrels, who are quick to take the birds' places at the feeders when they fly off, jump from eucalyptus to pine and are seemingly always at play.

Our yard is a virtual forest that we share with a family of deer who often come around to rest on our patio and to see if there is any interesting vegetation on which to feed. I've heard complaints from fellow Montclair residents who are livid about the deer "ruining" their expensive gardens and admit I was heartbroken to lose the blossoms off my recently transplanted hibiscus plant last summer. But my reaction was short-lived.

I realized that the deer were here first and that fragrant, fushia-colored hibiscus flowers and their shiny green leaves were probably a delicacy they couldn't resist. The leaves grew back. But the plant never flowered again.

It was killed in the frost of last winter.

Gardening has taught me a lot not only about other living things, but also about myself. For one, I've learned that I have the ability to be obsessive. Ever since the day I planted a hundred Asian lily bulbs and they began to protrude urgently through the soil, I don't think I've returned home from work, play or errands and walked inside the house before counting the sprouts and marking their growth.

There are forty-eight so far in the front yard and thirty-something in the back.

I've learned from my garden that the sweet smell of jasmine makes me nostalgic for warm summer nights in southern Illinois—a place I was more than ready to leave. I've learned that my affinity for the color purple goes beyond inanimate objects like clothing and wallpaper. Abundant crops of sage, alyssum, purple robe, petunias and pansies will attest to this.

And, in spite of my husband's proclamation that gardening is "simply trial and error," I've learned that I can help almost anything grow with constant care and attention.

Gardening has also reminded me that I have a real stupid-streak when it comes to harming my body. Let's just say that I've learned to wear sturdy leather gloves to avoid blisters on my hands and permanently stained fingernails.

Every afternoon at the hottest part of the day, the fog rolls away for a while allowing the powerful sunrays to burst through. They dry the dew from the flowers and the moisture from this drought-ravaged soil.

I'm usually away from my garden at this time, busy with other activities.

But I return home along with the fog and once again count my lilies and marvel at this growing, living thing I help to create every day.

Xeriscape

Leaving my California garden behind in 1993, I moved to northern Wisconsin. There I started from scratch in soil so fine and so grainy, that it could be packaged and sold as sandbox sand. Moving from "hardiness zone" nine where the common houseplants I had in pots while growing up in the Midwest stayed outside and grew into massive shrubs, to zone three, where the growing season lasts about as long as afternoon picnic, was fairly shocking to my personal ecosystem.

Alas, I had moved to the "Snow belt," and quickly learned the meaning of a short growing season. In the "Snow belt," that white stuff begins falling as early as September and today, which happens to be April Fool's Day, six inches fell this morning. No joke.

So, for my main gardens I learned to stick with perennials—plants and flowers I count on to come back year after year. In California annuals might be more appropriately named "forevers;" however, in Wisconsin they're simply a waste of money. To avoid frostbite they shouldn't be planted until Memorial Day weekend and by Labor Day they look like aged souls. Nevertheless, each spring I make a pilgrimage (a ten mile drive) to the neighborhood nursery known as "Benjamin's Greenery." At Benjamin's I stock up on geraniums or pansies and petunias—whatever catches my eye—to fill a few whiskey kegs and wheelbarrows with color to mark the summer season.

Aside from digging in the dirt and getting my nails dirty—because I still need incentive to wash the dishes—the trip to the nursery is the best part of the process. Benjamin's is a small, family-run business that makes me feel as though I'm shopping in someone's backyard. And, well, it actually *is* located in someone's backyard.

The proprietor is a beautiful woman named Dottie and I decided years ago that I want to be her when I grow up. She has long silver hair (I don't know how long since she always wears it tied in a simple, loose bun) and a serene face punctuated by gardener's eyes—a watery Caribbean blue. She wears an apron, of course, and is usually the first person I see when I walk inside the main greenhouse.

During the summer when I was pregnant with my second daughter, Camille, I made several trips to the nursery. With my nesting instincts at high tide, I planted and planted until the soil shouted back at me, "enough!" One day when I waddled into Benjamin's, Dottie looked up, perhaps surprised to see me again, and said, "Ah, I see you're still working on it."

"My garden or my baby?" I asked.

"We're always working on our gardens, dear," she said eyeing my protruding belly and touching me gently on the shoulder.

In Wisconsin I no longer refer to the flowers surrounding my home as my foggy garden, but rather, as my summer garden. By mid-July it's in full bloom and it's beautiful. There's very little work to be done besides weeding—because with gardening it's always about weeding. Weeding is to gardening what paperwork is to running a business. And dandelions, in particular, are like bookkeeping. They simply come with the territory and you have to keep pulling them up before things get out of control. Dandelions can spread a bad reputation across your garden as quickly as a bounced check.

And then there's the creeping charlie! Damn that creeping charlie. Its haughtier name is *Glechoma hederacea* and I understand it's also called ground ivy or creeping jenny. I swear loudly at a guy named "Charlie!" each time those hairy, kidney-shaped leaves with the small purple flowers creep into my garden beds. Keeping it under control is more annoying than walking to the mailbox and finding nothing but bills.

A better job than weeding is the mid-summer night's staking of my six-foot, purple, white and blue delphiniums. I love delphiniums. I once went to an Internet site to answer a few questions to determine what type of dog I'd be—which turned out to be a Golden Retriever—but if a gardening site existed with the sole purpose of comparing humans to plants, I'd be a delphinium. (Katharine Hepburn may have once told Barbara Walters that she was an oak tree, but I'm claiming the periwinkle delphinium.) The delphiniums in my garden are truly my pride and joy. Each July resort guests and fellow gardeners (especially from the Chicago area) ask how I grow them so tall. I simply attribute it to the sandy soil and throw in a little long, cold winter. (Sometimes you have to go the extra mile to make life in the Snow Belt seem attractive.) The truth is I have no clue how or why they grow as tall as corn stalks. The Chicago gardeners, all of whom are far more knowledgeable and experienced than I, assure me in rather condescending tones that "they won't last." Perhaps they won't. But for nearly nine seasons, they've come back graceful and majestic and send me running for maximum height bamboo poles that some of the resort guests eye up for potential fishing rods.

These days I leave Wisconsin before the end of the growing season and haven't been able to cut down the growth and mulch appropriately. So, I feel as though my garden is very untended. But since our Wisconsin home is located in a thick forest of trees, I count on the leaves to drop by October and swaddle the plants like blankets and protect them from another harsh winter while I soar with the rest of the snowbirds to the desert southwest. The lack of fall maintenance is starting to show and I find that each year my summer garden grows a little wilder.

As for gardening in the desert, I was a miserable failure. There's just no sense to the plan-free, trial-and-error theory when trying to grow plants in red, parched clay.

Fancying myself an erudite student of anything, I read lots of books and learned how to pronounce the word "xeriscape" (zero-scape) and soon understood it didn't mean dealing with lifeless, leafless plants—except, of course, for when there was a problem with the irrigation system. Even plants requiring little water still need a few drops in a climate where in the summer, eggs will fry on the sidewalk as early as breakfast. But I am an erudite flop with a shelf full of colorful books with mud stained pages. After making too many mistakes and losing too many expensive plants, we did the smart thing and hired a landscape architect and someone else to dig through this cement they call soil.

Today we may have a beautiful and colorful backyard oasis in our little

The Things I Wish I'd Said

corner of the Sonoran desert; however, since I didn't get my hands dirty though the final plotting, I feel this garden doesn't really belong to me.

And it's never seen a foggy day in its life.

House Ghost

June 30, 1992

There's a ghost outside my bedroom window. It gave me quite a start last night.

I had just come home from a softball game. Exhausted, I deposited my dirty clothes at the foot of the bed in a heap, just like a child—or from what my girlfriends tell me, just like most of our husbands. I threw myself onto the bed, gathered my favorite ten pillows and got comfortable.

Then, just as I reached for my favorite zebra-striped blanket, I saw something move.

My first instinct was to grab the blanket as fast as I could and cover myself up to my protruding, frightened eyeballs. I didn't want the eyeballs of any stranger to see me in the buff.

Meanwhile, I tried to focus on the elusive object while my heartbeat increased to the pace it had kept earlier on the softball field.

The television was on in the living room. It cast an eerie blue light through the picture window and into the yard. I thought maybe I had only seen a shadow and at once felt that silly feeling of overreaction.

I startle easily. Always have.

Ask anyone who works with me. When I'm sitting at the computer, I tune out—or rather, try to tune out the world. (This newspaper office can get quite hectic.) Whenever someone innocently walks up behind me and calls my name or taps my shoulder, it feels like an electric shock.

The Things I Wish I'd Said

I've been known to pop out of my chair and suck wind so hard it sounds like an opera note.

"Sorry, sorry, the offender usually says. Others, those who perhaps find it odd that someone can concentrate so intensely on her work, just screw up their faces and ask, "What's wrong with you?" I've even heard the words, "You look like you've just seen a ghost!"

So, I can imagine what my face looked like last night as it continued to peer out the bedroom window in search of the backyard ghost.

Our backyard is very secluded. We can't even get back there unless we walk through the house. I've yet to see an unknown human being, neighbor or stranger, through my windows. That's why we keep the curtains open.

We like having the view of the trees and the birds. We especially like it when the deer come to visit, which they do quite often.

Two days after I returned from a five-week safari in Africa, I woke up to find one of our deer friends with her wet, black nose pressed to the glass of our bedroom window. I think she was interested in the contents of our flower box for breakfast, and had I not raised my head in time, she might have fed from it like a trough.

After seeing so many antelope in Kenya—ten or so varieties—I felt very comfortable having this deer so close. She didn't startle me and I wouldn't have minded sharing my impatiens with her.

But I knew there was no deer outside my window last night. And it wasn't just a television shadow. Because again I saw this strange thing move. It was a slow movement, graceful like a dancer. Yet, through the fog, moving fast with the night wind, I could see that its movements were irregular— graceful and sharp. A jazz dancer.

Its color was not white, but pale—like sand or a peach. And it was large.

I wrapped the zebra-striped blanket around me like a shawl and rose from the bed. I stepped toward the window and pressed my forehead to the cold glass.

Just then, the "thing" let out a noise as loud as a clap and a gust of wind left the dripping remnants of a wet fog cloud on my window. I almost let out that opera note until all at once, it dawned on me: It was no ghost. It was a sheet. A stupid, silly and totally cliché sheet.

I sat back down on the bed and regathered my favorite ten pillows. I laughed because I had forgotten about the new clothesline. You see, I drained my savings account to fly to Africa and lost a month's worth of income. As a result, we've established all kinds of ways to cut household expenses. Hanging our clothes and linens out to dry instead of using the Maytag was just one idea. I guess we forgot the part about bringing them back inside.

This domestic stuff can be a little scary.

And it Gets Scarier

I still startle easily and imagine I always will.

Just the other morning, a Sunday, my daughter Willow thought it was a good idea to hide behind a wall and watch me work for awhile, which I tend to do before the kids get up. All at once she jumped out and yelled "RAH!" scaring the coffee cup right out of my hand. I spilled decaf all over the floor and wasn't happy about it. It took me an hour to get over being cross. In fact, I still feel terrible that I yelled at her.

Geez! And I thought domestic life was scary before I had children!

Kids can put the fear of God into you on any given day. And I don't just mean when they sneak up on you and make you drop your coffee. Take for instance the time I lost my toddler for five minutes just outside a grocery store in northern Wisconsin. Five minutes can feel like five hours when a state of panic like that takes over your every thought.

"How could she get away so fast?"

"I swear, I only turned my head for a second!"

"Oh my GOD! Will her face be on a milk bottle next month?"

"Will I be on the evening news begging for the return of my beautiful baby?"

"Could this really be happening to ME?"

Willow was barely a year old when it happened. She had only recently ventured off her knees and away from her coffee table prop and across the living room for the first time. Prior to that day, she was never outside my grasp. But on that day, I learned the meaning of baby mobility and the true meaning of that overused phrase, "the fear of God."

I was at the bank. Juggling a bundle of papers, letters, crap—and my baby—I opted to set her on the floor while I completed my brief transaction at a satellite teller window in a mall area outside the grocery store. I had placed her at my feet many times before and didn't suspect anything would happen. But in the time it took to hand the teller my deposit ticket and have her return a receipt, Willow disappeared. I simply looked down and she was gone.

Poof. Set baby down. Baby disappears.

As I paced wildly up and down the corridor of the mall, I had every available body within shouting distance searching for a "little girl with a head full of white curls and a blue jean jacket." And within a few minutes, a kind gentleman with my smiling child in his arms walked through the automatic glass doors from outside and said, "is this what you're looking for?"

I grabbed my daughter, thanked the man and then collapsed on the first bench I could find and cried. Sweet little Willow, with those precious, unbelievably blonde curls and round, absolutely kissable cheeks, stared at me wondering what could possibly be the matter. Meanwhile, a woman who had been stuffing polyester-filled animals into a vending machine—the kind where you try to snare a prize with a claw and that prize tends to escape the grasp of the claw until you've dropped in about five bucks worth of quarters—witnessed the panicky search for the missing toddler, and at once came up to us with the ugliest purple dragon you've ever seen and offered it to my daughter. It had black spots, a yellow T-rex crown of felt thorns and an orange tongue. Willow grabbed the horrid creature, named it "Dragon," and didn't let go of it for three years. After many sneak washings, sewing needle surgeries with whatever color of thread happened to be handy, as well as miles of U-turns back to the restaurant or store where she had left it, we finally had to wean Willow from her Dragon. I wish I could say we buried it somewhere, but it still sits on a shelf inside her bedroom closet and will forever serve as a reminder of how much I don't ever want to lose my child.

I've since learned that many mothers have experienced the alarm of escaping toddlers. These are mothers who own "leashes" and offer to loan them to you after you tell the story of how your kid got away. The leash I accepted had a stuffed Mickey Mouse head tethered to a coiled wire, like an old telephone receiver line, and Velcro straps for both Mom's wrist and toddler's wrist. My daughter took one look at the decapitated Mickey Mouse and his dirty yellow Velcro strap and as if to say, "yeah, right," ripped open the Velcro and tossed that mouse over her shoulder. I should have known better. After all, this was the same kid, who at the age of seven months, figured out how to open up the kitchen cabinets in spite of the safety locks.

It's pretty obvious to my husband and me—or anyone who meets Willow—that in addition to being very pretty, shes one smart little girl.

And there's nothing scarier than that.

The Desire To Be Homeless

November 26, 1991

Gary and John are leaving California. By the time this is published, they will be gone.

Gary (a nickname for Margaret) is five months pregnant with the couple's first child. John, who is originally from the Chicago area, is taking his wife and unborn child back to the place where he was born. Neither wants to raise a child in the state of California. They want a flat lot and a sense of community they say doesn't exist in Marin County. They also want their child to know his grandparents.

So, they're traveling by car and going east. A new home awaits them in Highland Park, Illinois. Jobs and business opportunities have been arranged. Family members, future baby-sitters, anticipate their return to the fold. They have sold some possessions, given away others. Movers carefully packed the furnishings and knickknacks they chose to take with them.

Gary and John are excited about this move. One might even say they're psyched. They thought about everything long and hard. And in their minds, everything about it is right.

Well, almost everything.

There's one thing weighing them down. It's their house. They certainly can't take it with them to Illinois. And in this stagnant economy, they can't sell it either.

"This house is killing us," said Gary. "We don't need it any more. We don't want it any more."

The Things I Wish I'd Said

Gary has been waking up in the middle of the night in angst over this three-plus bedroom, two bathroom real estate listing. "We made all the decisions about this move," she said. "We tied up all our loose ends and have our plans intact. But we have this house!"

I went to see this house last weekend. It's in Larkspur, nestled against the serene and majestic King Mountain, with a spectacular view of the valley. It's the kind of view that makes you want to keep your nose pressed to the glass of the sliding doors until your warm breath clouds the scene.

It's a beautiful house. They've owned it for four years and have put a lot of work into it. I couldn't help but say to them over and over, "This place will sell." There's got to be somebody out there who can still afford to buy a house.

It has only been on the market four months. But Gary and John have yet to receive an offer. In their frustration, they blame the realtors for giving them a false sense of optimism about the market. They also feel buyers aren't motivated to purchase right now. "There's so much to see," said John.

Meanwhile, they are willing to rent it to help pay the mortgage while they take on the new expense of a baby and a rented house in one of the Chicago area's more exclusive communities.

"At this point," said John, always the optimist, "whoever comes first—a renter or buyer—wins. But they've got to come soon."

Gary and John are among the many who are suddenly leaving California to live in other states. According to *Time* magazine's recent portrait, "California, The Endangered Dream," 510,000 have "escaped" in the past twelve months.

Admittedly the baby is ninety-five percent of their reason for leaving; however, Gary, a native of New Jersey, also mentioned the drought, traffic, earthquakes, fires and the high cost of living as reasons to get out. "And I don't like looking at brown hillsides," she said. "I'm tired of all the hot."

When I pointed out that she's moving to Chicago in the midst of the teeth-freezing temperatures of winter, she immediately came back with: "Well, nobody moves to Chicago for the weather."

No kidding.

Gary and John, both thirty-four years old, met in California, fell in love, got married and bought a piece of the California dream. Since the baby came into the picture, they realized that the dream they want to recreate is comprised not of geography, but of family.

There's just that one, expensive loose end: A house for which they worked so hard to attain. It has now become a half-million dollar burden.

We should all be so blessed.

The Burden of Real Estate

Gary and John sold their home a short time later and now live happily ever after in the Chicago suburbs with their three children. And that first child who they thought would be a boy? Surprise! No penis. No boy. They didn't get a boy until the third try.

Real estate is a fickle business. When we shopped for our first home in California just a few months after walking down the aisle and saying, "I do," we carried ourselves over the threshold and into a "seller's market." A house in the Oakland hills was a hot commodity, and the competition to get one was just short of cutthroat. Well-heeled real estate agents had offices on every corner of Montclair village and raced through closing papers like kids whipping through stacks of homework in order to go outside and play. Buyers attending open houses were greeted at the door not with the smell of freshly baked bread and a business card but with smug proclamations from selling agents like "this house already has a strong offer with two backups and will most likely result in a bidding war." In other words, "Move on kid. You don't stand a snowball's chance."

The house we bought, a mere cottage by normal house standards, listed at a price we could afford, which therefore made it affordable to a lot of first time homebuyers looking for a nice view of San Francisco Bay. We put in our offer for the asking price on the day the house went on the market. In that market, she told us, everything we'd ever learned about purchasing real estate from our parents was pure nostalgia. Coming in with a low-ball offer or anything less than the asking price was not only unheard of and impolite, it was stupid. Then she led us to believe we "won" the house over the other offers because of her savvy techniques and experience as an I'm-gonna-get-things-done-and-smile-all-the-way-to-the-bank-with-five-percent-of-the-sale-in-my-pocket kind of gal.

She was in celebration mode the night she called with the news. I heard bubbles in her voice and the clink of a champagne glass hitting her teeth. (Pocketing five-figures for a few hours work was certainly something to celebrate.) "There were three offers for the asking price," she said. "But they gave it to us because I was smart enough to say we'd have all our inspections and financing in order in three weeks."

Clearly, she was a genius of a buying agent. All agents seem like geniuses to first time home buyers who walk through the doors of their new homes in the giddy afterglow of finding a match and the heady confusion of writing a series of big, big checks and scratching signatures on thousands of lines next to cellophane sticky notes reading "sign here." Handing new homeowners the key to their castle and a one-year home warranty "gift" along with a philodendron in a green plastic pot with a big yellow bow is the easy part of any agent's job.

Acting as a selling agent, however, is a different role requiring a different kind of savvy. Selling agents must wear a mask of much thicker skin because when a property doesn't sell, their clients blame them. Having only experienced the buying side of a deal, we didn't know this.

When we decided to move we asked our perky, can-do agent to list the house. We had hoped to stay at least as long as the recommended five years, but before we knew it, it was our turn to join the Exodus and leave California to return to the seasonal world known as the Midwest. Three years was a short time but many changes took place in the real estate market during that period. Some liked to blame the seven-year drought or the massive fire in 1991 that wiped out a substantial portion of our urban forest community. Others blamed the economy and attached jingles to the mix by saying things like "the bottom has fallen out of the housing market." Ultimately it was a simple matter of bad timing and bad luck. We purchased our little house in a seller's market and we intended to sell it in a buyer's market. If our crystal ball worked we would have known that if we held on through the dot-com boom of the 1990s, we would have made a fortune on our little cottage. But this was not the case.

Did I already suggest that real estate is a fickle business?

Our effervescent real estate professional, who wore a graduate's mortarboard as a buying agent but exchanged it for a dunce cap when acting the role of selling agent, wasn't ready to give up the days of the quick buck. And we were greedily game to help her make it.

On the day she came up the hill to our cottage and witnessed all the changes and improvements we had made—installing hardwood floors and adding French doors to the living room, remodeling the bathroom with decorative, Mexican tile, updating the kitchen—her eyes blinked up and down like an old-fashioned cash register, and the calculator in her mind added and added. She valued our house with seller's market criteria and like everyone else who tends to believe their property is worth more than it really is, we let her. And what we experienced in the big, bad market was not unlike the young, rash pig brothers who built their houses of sticks and straw. Agents who *were* paying attention to market trends snubbed us with "who-do-you-think-you are?" scoffs at our open houses, and their sighs seemed like huffs and puffs as they blew our hopes down. Neighbors we barely knew came by to see what on earth we did to make our little piece of real estate so valuable. Since this was the post Proposition Thirteen era and our selling price no longer had any impact on the real estate taxes in our hillside neighborhood, half our neighbors hoped we'd get our asking price so their own homes would earn higher appraisals. The other half of our neighbors, those who had been in the neighborhood for years and because of Howard Jarvis's 1978 version of the Boston Tea Party, paid about five cents in property taxes, snickered and called us naïve.

Prior to the passage of Proposition Thirteen—commonly known as Prop 13—which limited California property taxes to an annual increase of one percent of the market value and limited assessment hikes to two percent, many residents on fixed incomes were being taxed right out of their homes. Jarvis claimed he witnessed a lady in Los Angeles suffer a heart attack at the county assessor's office when she couldn't convince them to lower her taxes so she could still afford to live there.

Prop. 13 reduced California state tax revenues from $11 billion in 1978 to $6 billion in 1979. While the state found other ways to collect taxes with sales tax revenues, for example, which grew nearly fifteen percent during the same time period, it wasn't long before Prop. 13 opponents made it the ridiculous scapegoat for everything from the collapsed highway caused by the 1989 Loma Prieta earthquake, to closing libraries to even the failure to convict O.J. Simpson on murder charges in 1994!

I know *we* didn't blame Prop. 13 when our house didn't sell immediately. Like our friends Gary and John before us, we blamed our real estate agent.

Gary and John mentioned a "false sense of optimism" delivered by their agent; but we thought our agent had a false sense of the market, making us lose potential early sales by pricing it too high. And we were anything but optimistic. We knew our pretty little cottage would sell eventually, but we had to face that we wouldn't make back the money we put into it and would be lucky to break even.

When the three-month exclusive-right-to-sell contract was about to expire and the moving van had been filled, other area agents swooped down on us like vultures, all with suggestions as to how *they* could sell the place overnight. "Drop your price," said most. "Paint your bedroom walls," said another. One even suggested we put down new carpeting in the living room over the beautiful hardwood floors we had recently installed.

These agents expected us to pump more money into a place we were ready to leave to the next home improvement crew, knowing we had virtually no equity built up after three years. All they saw was their potential commissions and could care less about us.

Being on the selling side of a real estate transaction made me very wary of real estate agents. Those with eager buyers called at all hours of the day and night to request a showing and then often failed to come at the designated time. Many showed up unannounced, catching me just out of the shower or in some other unpresentable state, and expected me to step aside or attach myself to the wall like tacky artwork so their clients could sniff their way through my closets.

The house was no longer ours. It was like road kill exposed to predators in search of commissions, and I couldn't wait to get out of there.

Ultimately we stayed with our original agent, and as we waved goodbye and headed east we said, "Sell it. Do whatever it takes."

It took about five months and as predicted, we received less than what we had originally paid. But, of course, it sold. Every real estate agent will tell you it only takes one buyer. And a buyer came along, a lawyer, who along with his lawyer wife, closed quite a deal. And a few months later when their pretty Mexican-tiled bathroom floor flooded and they had to endure a big plumbing expense, they tried to get us to fork over the cost of the repair. "Our plumber said there was no way you could not have known about the plumbing problem and you're in violation of the disclosure law," read the letter typed on attorney's letterhead. Indeed, we were aware of the problem in the bathroom and in a return letter referred the lawyers-in-love to the disclosure statement we provided with the sale where on line sixteen we checked the YES box regarding known plumbing problems, and notated regular Roto-Rooter maintenance to clear out the zealous ivy roots invading the underground pipes.

We weren't putting another dime into that house.

Five years later during the boom in the Silicon Valley when real estate prices escalated in sync with the Nasaq numbers, one of our neighbors sold his place for twice as much as we did. In light of what happened to the dot-com failures a few years after that when the bottom dropped out of the technology market, I can only wonder what's going on with prices of houses in our old neighborhood today. Perhaps I should call a few Bay Area real estate agents and listen for bubbles in their voices.

As for our ongoing experience in the world of real estate, we have had positive experiences as both buyers and sellers. Selling, however, has always been a more difficult task.

Aah, the burden of real estate. It's a blessing *and* a curse.

Chapter 2

Let's Just Talk About ME

"Guided by my heritage of a love of beauty and

a respect for strength—in search of my

mother's garden, I found my own."

—Alice Walker, *In Search of Our Mothers' Gardens*

Beauty Queens and War Heroes

July 2, 1991

I'm not sure why it surprised me to learn that there are still things in this world like beauty pageants. But sure enough, there are and it did.

As I heard a brief account on the radio the other day about the new Miss California, I realized that Miss California, Miss America and, good heavens, Miss Universe are still out there with their showy smiles and tiaras glistening for all to see.

Knowing that women are still awarded lavish titles and prizes based on the randomness of chromosomes and their abilities to answer questions without offending any popular interest groups is as disturbing to me as the recent rash of right-to-life legislation limiting a woman's right to choose her reproductive fate.

What really bothers me, however, is this: The new Miss California reportedly sang a Disney song as her talent and proclaimed General Norman Schwarzkopf as her hero.

Now, I have no idea what this woman looks like, but I can only assume that it's something like a Barbie Doll—or any kind of wind-up doll programmed to say what the buying public wants to hear.

Well Miss California, now that you have your crown and your scholarship and whatever else Mickey Mouse and Stormin' Norman helped you achieve; I'd like to ask you another question.

How do you feel about General Schwarzkopf's intention to permanently limit women's roles in the military to non-combat positions? By basically proclaiming women as inferior beings he said the U.S. military would be "disadvantaged if women were in combat against all-male foreign armies." Schwarzkopf prefaced his statements by saying that he was "very much in favor of women's rights, but . . . "

I don't think women will ever be truly equal in this country until we get rid of those "buts", the non-empathetic (i.e. macho) men who continually make decisions for us, and the women who blindly worship these men.

Wouldn't it have been great if the new Miss California was a part-time construction worker (working her way through school) who installed a set of double doors as her talent and proclaimed Gloria Steinem as her hero(ine)? I would have even settled for a hero like Ralph Nader or Stevie Wonder.

As a pre-teen I admit I used to watch beauty pageants on TV as eagerly as the annual showing of *Cinderella* or *The Wizard of Oz*. Like many awkward, flat-chested young girls with overbites and frizzy hair, perhaps these parades of beautiful women, perfect as the Barbie dolls with which I played, gave me hope for the future.

I longed for the day when the boys at school would stop teasing me with names like "board," "flatsie," and the ever-popular "carpenter's dream." I was so accustomed to the ridicule that when somebody called me a "virgin," in spite of my Catholic upbringing, I was sure that it was something bad. (The nuns never actually told us what a virgin was. And when I asked my dad what it meant, he said that it was the Virgin Mary's first name.)

Thank goodness I survived puberty and the Catholic church, and paid attention to what was going on in the world of the mid-1970s along the way.

The last thing I remember about beauty pageants prior to my recent exposure is that there were women's activist groups picketing against female exploitation in front of the auditorium. I remember this made me feel good and, for the first time, proud to be a woman. I was beginning to understand power and that it didn't matter if you were a boy or a girl, a man or a woman, beautiful or awkward. When being "judged," what mattered was your ability to formulate opinions, express your ideas and believe that you had something to offer.

Today, I'm afraid that in my little bubble of confidence I've ignored what's still (or once again?) going on out there as young girls continue to idolize beauty queens and war heroes while our fragile "equal" rights are sliding the wrong way on the proportion scale.

It seems our country is lapsing into *Leave-it-to-Beaver* withdrawal symptoms as fewer women and men want to struggle with the laborious intoxication of revolution and the accomplishment of "having it all."

Sure, we've come along way, baby—and all that. But let's face it. This may be California, but we do not, and never will live in Disney World.

It's All About How You Look

On the day this column ran, my editor received a complaint via telephone that had something to do with my picture—a grainy black and white headshot that appeared above my column each week. The caller said I was "too pretty" to make the commentary put forth in my column.

To this day I don't think I heard my editor correctly.

I guess it's fair to say there are certain sentences I cannot comprehend. When anyone speaks of my appearance, for example, I simply stop listening. Telling me I am pretty has the same effect on me as telling me I'm short—or Russian. In my mind, it's just not true.

Let me make this perfectly clear: Girls once labeled "gawky" who insisted songs like Janis Ian's self-pitying anthem, "At Seventeen", were clearly written for them, don't ever believe they're pretty. It doesn't take a Freudian psychologist to understand that if you're told time after time during your formative years that you're dorky or ugly, or if you at one point acquired enough stinging nicknames based on your appearance to start turning around when people shouted them at you from behind, a certain negative self-image will always be a part of your reality.

I admit that by the time I turned seventeen I had a sort of metamorphosis, but I attribute that to growing boobs and getting my braces off on the same day. I wasn't completely pathetic for all four years of high school, since in the latter half I attended a few dances and didn't miss my senior prom. Fortunately I entered college with a lot of self-protective armor—leaving the name-callers and those with knowledge of my awkward youth behind—and presented myself as a strong, smart and yes, ugh, pretty young woman.

But adolescent/teenage ridicule is a little like acne. It leaves permanent scars. And I'd give anything to shield my daughters from this kind of scar tissue.

Last night, my seven-year-old asked the kind of question that only a seven-year-old can ask. "Mom," she said, "why do we grow?"

I took the bait and dove into a Girl Scout explanation of the pituitary gland, pointing to the place where hers is located. As I moved to the topics of estrogen and menstruation, she cocked her head like a dog responding to a high-pitched whistle, and listened intently. Knowing my bright little girl, she retained every word. "But why do we have to bleed?" she asked.

At this I wrapped my full-grown arms around her and held her small, skinny frame close to mine. I thought about how young, precious and truly brief this phase of her life is. (I'm still trying to figure out how she got to be seven so fast!) We don't know this as children, of course, but most of us spend the better portion of our lives as adults; yet we are ultimately products of our youthful experiences. And I don't think we realize it until we raise children, but a child's mind is incredibly keen. They are like sponges soaking in everything around them, and it takes a long time before some things get squeezed out. As much as we want to create individual utopias for our children, protect them from all the ills of a society that tends to hate you if you're beautiful—and hate you even more if you're ugly—we must face that they're going to eventually get mired in some nasty stuff.

My daughter looked up at me, a perfect full moon face with a huge, gaping hole where her front tooth was just as recently as last week and issued a trusting smile. Part of me couldn't help but think, "She's doomed."

Michele VanOrt Cozzens

In giving her life, I've recreated myself. Each time she jumps rope ahead of us during our morning stroll to the bus stop, I see a pair of legs that look more like arms dance over the rope and I wonder if she'll have the same nicknames as I. "Legs" and / or "Leggy", maybe even the unfortunate "daddy long legs."

When it comes to discussing "growing up" with my daughters, I intend to answer every question they throw at me. (Even unexpected questions like, "Mom, what is light bulb suction?") I was fortunate to have older sisters who explained life issues to me because my mother was unavailable in that department. I remember her racing to the television to turn off any commercial advertising products like feminine napkins or, heaven forbid, douche, because to her it simply wasn't proper. Just once I wish she would have assured me that when the braces came off, I'd have a beautiful smile or that when the rest of my body eventually grew to fit my knock-kneed daddy-long-legs, the name-calling would stop. She *did* say more than once that it was better to have skinny legs than fat legs but somehow that wasn't good enough.

Knowledge breeds confidence. If my daughters are equipped with the knowledge that they *will* grow out of their awkward stages and become beautiful, intelligent women—women who could eventually find more useful ways to spend their money than on light bulb *or* liposuction—hopefully they'll politely respond with a "thank you" each time someone compliments their appearance instead of turning off like an electrical plug with a short circuit.

I suppose the bottom line here is that ten years ago I wouldn't have said this, but today I feel that if either of my daughters wishes some day to enter a beauty pageant and sing a Disney song in order to obtain a crown and a scholarship, I wouldn't object. I mean, I'd cringe, but I probably wouldn't give them a hard time. (It is a mother's job to support her children, but a mother's right to cringe.) Why, just the other day when my kindergartener announced that she wanted to be in cheerleading, I nearly fell off my chair. First of all, I didn't know they made cheerleaders out of five-year-olds. Secondly, I thought of one of my lifelong regrets in having wasted my best high school athletic years on the sidelines in a short skirt. I almost launched into a history of Title IX (about as interesting as my speech on the pituitary gland) and how when I was a young girl we didn't have the opportunity to be much besides cheerleaders; however, I chose a hopeful tone and asked my darling Camille if she wouldn't rather be the one playing the sport instead of the one yelling about it on the sidelines.

She looked at me like I was cracked. "Mom," she said, "I like the uniform."

Once again my five-year-old proved to me that more often than not, it's all about how you look.

New Age Golf Pro—Part One

The first time my father saw me swing a golf club he was convinced I'd be the next Babe Didrickson. "She's a natural," he bragged. "When she connects with that devil, it goes a mile."

I was thirteen with a body the shape of a nine iron. But I was athletic. I'd try any sport. Golf was intriguing to me mostly because my father spent a lot of time playing it. And he had a great golf bag, which was filled with more colorful toys than an Easter basket. Three of the tallest clubs were covered with knit blue caps. They were soft and warm like well-cared-for children.

One summer day I remember I decided to "play golf." So I smuggled one of my dad's clubs into the front yard. Clutching the handle, I held my arms out straight and allowed the club to lead me like the forked stick of a water witch.

When I found the ideal spot I lowered the club to the ground and imagined a small white target. "Shhhh," I said to the singing birds. I'd seen enough golf on television to know that whispering was important. And then I started swinging.

"Hey," called my father suddenly as I froze with fear. "Let me see how you're holding that club."

I timidly showed him my white knuckles. "It sort of hurts," I admitted.

"No wonder," laughed Dad. "You're holding it wrong. Let me show you."

The Things I Wish I'd Said

He took the driver from my hands and executed a long-winded, step-by-step demonstration. He said I should lock my pinky and index fingers, aligning my thumbs along a natural line.

Finally he handed me the club and I gripped it appropriately.

Then, under the scrutinizing glare of his intense blue eyes, I went into a slow, controlled backswing. Before I finished the swing, I looked up to see if he was watching with approval.

"Keep your head down," he cried.

"I'm sorry," I said. "Let me try again."

But he didn't let me. He grabbed the club and headed toward the garage saying something about it not being right for me. I thought he meant the game of golf.

Instantly, I labeled golf a stupid game. I envisioned his friends in their plaid, polyester slacks and silly hats chasing little balls around vast valleys of green. I thought of their wives sitting at home waiting for them while at the 19th hole, they drank beer and exaggerated putting distances like fishermen holding their hands out to show the lengths of their catch.

But my dad came back to me moments later with a different club. "Try this seven iron to practice your swing," he said. "It's got a shorter shaft." He also brought me a little plastic ball with lots of holes in it so I could practice hitting something. And I was immediately successful.

The best part, however, was my dad's smile. "With that swing, you'll be on the pro tour in no time and I'll be able to retire," he said.

The next day we went to the links. I was nervous as we stood on the first tee. Dad pointed into the enormous green field before us and said to look for the flag. I searched in vain while he teed up a "pink lady" golf ball. He reminded me to keep my head down. "Now don't try to kill it," he said. "Just swing through the ball."

I shifted my weight and swung with what I was sure was sheer grace. And then I looked to the sky expecting to see a pink streak heading toward that mysterious flag. But instead I saw only clouds.

"Where'd it go?" I asked.

My father pointed to the ground. "You missed," he said.

On my third miss, the look of disappointment on Dad's face about killed me. Visions of LPGA gold cups and blue ribbons were wiped from the mantelpiece in his mind as white golf carts gathered and stirred behind us like impatient chickens.

"We'll have to take you to the driving range for some practice," he said. "We can't hold up the next foursomes any longer."

And then he turned to his friends and said, "She thinks she's Babe Didrickson."

I thought he meant Babe Ruth and wanted to say that even Babe struck out swinging once in awhile. But I kept my head down and clutched my father's hand as he led me to the pro shop to buy a bucket of balls.

New Age Golf Pro—Part Two
February 18, 1992

Ever since my dad said I had the potential to be a golf pro like Babe Didrickson, I wondered who this woman was. It took a made-for-TV movie to figure it out. I don't remember much about the movie except that Alex Karras, the former NFL star, played her husband, George Zaharias.

Much like Zaharias pushed his wife to excel, I felt my dad pushed me a little too much to be more than I could be with a golf club in my hands. And like any red-blooded American teenager, I rebelled.

The truth is I wasn't that good. Sure, I'd occasionally connect on a drive, but you're nothing at the game of golf if you're not consistent.

I remember instances of tossing my club and walking off the green in a huff the same way I used to scramble Monopoly pieces when I didn't like the way the board game was going. I'm sure my allergy to grasses was formed on the golf course. It was a good excuse anyway to avoid accompanying my dad on his daily summer vacation excursions.

My parents live in a golfers' mecca. It's a retirement community in the Missouri Ozarks where at any given time a golf cart might scurry past their home on the way to the links. They play golf year round—rain being the only deterrent.

It's not often that I get to visit them; however, whenever I do, you can bet we play golf. I realized some six years ago that if I wanted to spend time with them on their turf, I had to give up my attitude toward golf.

I guess I'm not such a bad player after all. In fact, I can even see my potential to be a very good player. Still, I'm not that willing to dedicate my time to this game. And that is what it takes. Time.

Of course, it takes green fees too.

The good news is that all is not lost on me in the world of golf. Much to my surprise, and to my father's surprise as well, today I am a fairly well-known golfer. I am, in fact, a golf pro. I play on the pro circuit, have tournament victories under my belt and have even won some cash.

For those of you who have never heard of it, and be prepared to laugh because everyone else does, there's a fledgling sport out there known as disc golf. There are professional and amateur players worldwide, and nearly 10,000 of us are card-carrying members of the PDGA —the Professional Disc Golf Association.

Disc golf, a.k.a. Frisbee golf, is played on a disc golf course, and there are two of them in the Bay Area. There's a nine-hole course in Moraga and an 18-hole course in Berkeley.

Disc golfers carry bags filled with discs the same way ball golfers carry a bag filled with clubs. Some discs are drivers; some are putters. These are not the same Frisbee discs that you play catch with on the beach. They weigh somewhere around 175 grams and have sharp, aerodynamic edges. Some are heavier than others and are meant to fly different ways depending upon the obstacles between you and the target.

The target is a galvanized steel basket. It stands about four feet high. And it is our goal to get the disc from the tee and into the basket in as few throws as possible.

Yes, it's an odd game. Sometimes, when I find myself perched atop a cliff or surrounded by poison oak or raspberry brambles preparing to throw a molded petroleum product across some rugged landscape, I think myself to be a little crazy.

The bottom line is that disc golf is fun.

I started playing because I married a professional player. Since being a new age golf widow was not my idea of a good marriage, I tagged along to a few of his weekend tournaments. It was while caddying for him that I figured this game was something I might like to try.

So today, while most women my age are having and raising babies, I'm carrying around a sack of discs and wondering why they won't behave the way I want them to. I marvel at their smooth newness and feel awe at the whirring sound they make as they sail above my head. And when I inadvertently throw them against trees, I carefully smooth their cuts and promise to treat them better.

Our season begins this weekend with the fifth annual Caldecott Open. And I'll be there—ready to compete—a slightly different version of the golf pro my dad had once envisioned.

New Age Golf Pro—Part Three

How many times have I written about or explained the sport of disc golf over the years? Too many to count. Of course when I wrote these back-to-back columns I had no clue that I would someday be the owner of a disc golf resort, but that's what I left the newspaper world to do.

I'm pleased to report that the sport of disc golf is no longer something that makes people laugh as a first reaction. (It's gone from a full-fledged laugh to a mere snicker.) The number of members in the PDGA has amassed to over 20,000 and hundreds of courses have popped up across the country. When we officially established our disc golf course in northern Wisconsin in 1994, there were only six courses in the state. Today there are over forty. We are among the few who charge a green fee—since it obviously isn't on public property—and we didn't have help paying for the equipment with donations from the local Lions, Rotary or Optimist Clubs. (What is an Optimist Club anyway? Do they only let happy, upbeat people in?) But to help pay for our $10,000 equipment investment, last summer we collected over 1,500 green fees. We're not quite laughing all the way to the bank, but in a few more years our twenty-four hole course will be paid for and we will have had the pleasure of teaching the game to thousands of people.

My role in the world of disc golf has certainly evolved. I'm still a card-carrying pro, but now, since I'm over forty I'm considered a "Pro Master" and I rarely compete. I took the route of a lot of female athletes who find that once the babies are born, mixing competition and motherhood is like trying to compose classical music in a room full of transistors blaring country music on AM radio stations. Individual competition takes concentration. Any successful athlete—disc golfer or otherwise—will tell you that physical skill is only part of the game. It's the games you play inside your head that can beat you on any given day.

After giving birth, and what that does to your brain, all bets are off. You might as well attempt to compete in your chosen sport without wearing a bra because while your tits are bouncing all over the playing field, the part of your mind that isn't annoyed at losing the lean body you once had is worried about whether or not the babysitter is actually paying attention to your toddler instead of talking on the phone.

I don't know one mother who goes for more than five minutes without shifting a thought over to her child. Where is she now? How is she getting along? Is she safe? Is she smiling? Trying to concentrate on anything when there's a child around calling, "mommy, mommy, mommy" (whether you hear her or not) is simply a waste of time.

Athletes by definition are selfish. And when you become a mother, self no longer fits into the equation. After my first daughter was born I suggested tournament directors provide childcare when they complained that not enough women showed up at their tournaments, and vowed to always provide babysitting at the tournaments at our resort. For three years in a row, it cost me $150 for the weekend to play in the women's seed of a twelve-person team in the annual team tournament we host. Since only the top two teams finish in the money and our team ended up in third each time, professionally speaking it was time to sit out and let a younger, childless and more talented woman take my slot.

So, I did what any big shot has-been (or never was) golfer would do when it was time to relinquish the throne of the coveted women's seed position on the home team. I wrote to the current world champion and asked her to replace me.

Referring to Juliana as "more talented" is a feeble understatement. This gal is so good at the sport that she puts a huge portion of the men's open field to shame. (Even a sport born in the bosom of the Title IX-1970s can bring out the worst macho-schmuck nature in men.) There was a rumor going around for a short time that she kept a bedpost notch-type list of all the men she'd beaten over the years; however, she flatly denied this claim. A lot has been written about Juliana over the years, and by the way, in our world of flying molded petroleum products she needs no last name. She's like Cher. Or Madonna. One website article gave her the title, "Disc Golf Goddess." And I must say, I took a little offense to that supercilious moniker since I've written the words: "Mrs. Cozzens, Sandy Point Goddess," on the backs of my discs for years. But I suppose Juliana deserves the title more than I. I'm more like a matriarch than a goddess. Call me "The Old Woman and the Sea of Plastic." As a 1999 inductee to the Wisconsin Disc Golf Hall of Fame, I'm thinking of having a statue made of myself for display along side the list of my scant achievements, which depicts a big-breasted woman with children hanging out of her golf bag.

No, I never made it too far on the professional disc golf circuit. Just when I seemed to be at the top of my game, I traded in *my* toys for my children's toys. Playing disc golf while pregnant destroyed my backhand, which is the motion used most often for distance shots or drives. First of all, I couldn't fully reach around my basketball-sized gut, and when I released the disc, my belly wanted to follow and it threw me off balance like a top out of spin. During my pregnancies I learned to use a forehand motion, a shot I usually reserved for accuracy on approach shots. And I became pretty good at it by using newer, high-tech discs designed to be thrown in an "S-curve" for maximum distance. The problem was after the babies were born, I couldn't get the backhand to work anymore. On top of my feet growing into a whole new shoe size and the feeling of having had aliens take over my once slender and solid physique, my ability to grip the disc and release with a strong backhand snap simply disappeared.

I worked and worked at it, and by the time my youngest daughter was two, I had the backhand working again. But what I no longer had was the desire to compete.

Aside from occasional league play or doubles matches, the last real tournament I played in was the 2000 Sandy Point Team Invitational at our resort. My husband, the team captain, had hired a bunch of our old California pals as ringers and we invited seven other teams from Michigan, Minnesota, Illinois, Wisconsin and Texas, who were ready to take us down. I was in excellent physical shape; however, mentally I was a wreck. Nervous about impressing my California buddies, the guys who taught me the game, I didn't sleep the night before competition began. Then my babysitter (the one who cost me $150 for the weekend) was half-an-hour late, which gave me virtually no time to warm up. Each time I stepped outside of my house, ninety-five other competitors called my name in need of something only a tournament director (and resort host) could fulfill. And every time I stepped back inside the house, my little girls pulled the "mommy, mommy, mommy" routine I referenced earlier. I went upstairs to my private bathroom and away from my ten houseguests and fellow teammates and threw up.

The team tournament is a match-play event. Each team consists of twelve seeded players and players compete head-to-head with corresponding seeds from each team for twelve holes before moving onto the next match. It took me a twelve-hole match to calm down after my episode of worshiping the porcelain god (and believe me, I'd have rather been worshipping after a night of too much partying than because of stress!) and play *my* game. I had to remind myself that I helped design the course on which I competed and played every day for six weeks going into the event. Finally, I left thoughts of both my children *and* my former self behind and played a good, solid game of disc golf.

I had no regrets about hiring Juliana to take my place the following year. I joked to the team that I thought I found "an adequate replacement." And she posted an impressive 5-1-1 record—tying one of the same top pro women that I had tied the previous year. That was a sort of inadvertent feather in my retired cap.

These days I'm happy to get out and throw recreationally and give "lessons" to anyone who might ask for my help after buying discs in our pro shop. My daughter, Willow, (PDGA #9783) may be well on her way to becoming the next Juliana. She's got the form and enjoys the game. I see in her what my dad must have seen the day I first starting swinging a golf club in our front yard and I'll do my best to silently live vicariously through her and not push too hard.

As for Camille (PDGA #13,001), I'm not sure where her prowess will lie. When Camille was three years old, only a week after returning to the resort for the season, she was accidentally hit in the face with a golf disc at point blank range. I had left the girls on the golf course with a visiting friend, who suggested I go inside and start dinner while he looked after them. My husband was away for the weekend, acting as an assistant tournament director in another town. I had barely gotten the food out of the refrigerator when I heard alarming screams, and recognized the pitch as belonging to the one-and-only Hurricane Camille. At the front door I met up with too much blood streaming from the perfect face of my child, as she writhed in the arms of our very upset friend. "I only turned my head away for a second and Willow threw it sideways!" he said. Meanwhile, as he had protectively and instinctively scooped up Camille to bring her to me, he left Willow on the golf course. I didn't notice she was missing as I cleaned the gaping wound beneath Camille's big, blue, Precious-Moment eye, and when I strapped her into the car for the long drive to the emergency room, finally discovered that her older sister was nowhere to found.

A short search through the golf course found her hiding behind a tree on hole three, crying crocodile tears and shaking like an aspen leaf. "I'm sorry," she cried. "I just *yanked it* and I didn't mean to do it. Am I going to be punished? Are you ever going to let me play disc golf again?"

I didn't know for which child to feel sorrier. And further, I couldn't believe Willow used the term "yanked." As every disc golfer knows, a yank is when you hang on to the disc too long and release it so that it flies either behind you, or more often at a ninety-degree angle from your pivot foot. Anyone standing next to you is fair game—or as in Camille's case, a target for stitches.

Camille required five stitches and now has a permanent smile below her left eye. I keep hearing things like, "she's young and the scar will fade over time," and it doesn't bother her, but for me it's a constant reminder that there's danger around every corner and certainly next to every yank. Just more things to think about as I worry about my children.

Unlike me, Camille was a trooper during the procedure. I was calm getting her to the hospital as I explained what happened to three different people with clipboards in their hands and pencils behind their ears, admitting us and screening us for potential child abuse. But after they cleaned the wound and injected a local anesthesia into her face, by the second stitch I was toast. The assisting nurse, who had one eye on me throughout the process, noticed when I grabbed my abdomen and swallowed like I was going to let the lava flow. "Where's the bathroom?" I asked. This old pro led me to it and when I returned after simply throwing water on my face, she told me not to be embarrassed because it "happens all the time." She insisted I lie down on the bed next to my daughter and brought me a ginger ale to suck on through a straw.

When I next saw the faces of off-duty paramedics peering into the room to see the latest-mom-to-lose-it over-her-kid's-blood, I could only believe that I had come full circle in the world of disc golf.

Friendship

When I first met C.L., she didn't talk about her family very much. She didn't talk about much of anything besides softball.

We met at a softball game. Our boyfriends were playing; we were watching. She heard me mention to another spectator that I played on a women's softball team and boldly asked if she could play on the team too.

We had room for a good third base player, and she said she could fill the slot. The rest of the women on the team liked her, and soon she was part of the group. That's how we became friends seven years ago.

We didn't connect right away like some best friends do. We, as young adults freshly sprung into the world of choices, were wary of each other. At that point in our lives we both had been through good and bad relationships. My bumps and bruises came after an idyllic childhood that ended much too abruptly and deposited me in a world for which I wasn't prepared. C.L.'s came from a family that never stayed in one place and which, to her, never seemed quite right.

C.L. was a military brat. She and her four siblings were moved from Texas to Wisconsin to Illinois to Kansas. There was a stint in Italy and then it was back to Texas again before finally settling in Northern California. She made friends quickly in her new towns. But just as quickly, she found reasons to end the friendships before it was time to move. She didn't want anyone to get too close.

The Things I Wish I'd Said

When she met me, however, C.L. was ready to make friends—friends who would stick around. She and her boyfriend, both auto mechanics, had recently bought a home together and started a business fixing cars. She was putting down roots.

I liked the idea of knowing a female mechanic. I had never met a woman with grease-stained fingernails who could change the oil or weld the cracked tail pipe on my car just as easily as I could type a letter.

Ours was a childlike friendship. Always on the softball field, we were completely informal in our play clothes. We giggled and wrestled, turned cartwheels and raced each other. We'd scream out obscenities as though we had just learned these words and didn't care who heard us. Playing with C.L. reminded me of playing with the kids in the secure suburban neighborhood where I spent the first eighteen years of my life. One minute we'd fight over the rules of the game, the next we'd walk off the field arm-in-arm making fun of the players on the other team.

As we spent more time together during and after our weekly softball games, I learned little snippets of her life and bits and pieces about her family. I didn't ask too many questions because a part of me wanted to keep things light. And C.L.'s responses were anything but light.

Her mother was an alcoholic. Her parents divorced when she was a teenager—but then found their way back together and remarried a few years later. One of her sisters married at a young age and immediately had two children. When the marriage got ugly, she moved back to her parents' home. One of her brothers was gay. This was the only thing she had ever said about him until about a year later. The next thing I knew, he was dying of AIDS. And then he was dead. We never talked about it after that. At least not until recently, on the fifth anniversary of his death when C.L. finally said goodbye to him.

Today C.L. is married to her mechanic boyfriend and their business is thriving. She is mother to a curly-haired little girl, and yes, we still play softball together. We still laugh together, chase after balls and occasionally wrestle each other to the ground.

What has changed about our friendship is that C.L. and I have learned to cry together. At some point through the years, we started listening to each other. We have developed a mature friendship, which is not based on the coincidence of having much in common or being thrown into a situation like a neighborhood or a classroom.

Despite our late start, we gave each other a different view of youth. C.L. gave me back a playfulness I had left behind, and I gave her a stability she had never known.

Friendship Warped by Women's Weekend

I'm sorry to say I've lost touch with C.L. I haven't received a Christmas card from her in years and I'm sure we'll never be as close as we were when I wrote this piece. In the period that followed its publication, I grew more and more uncomfortable with what she wanted from me in our friendship, and found myself steadily pulling away from her.

C.L. had tried for years to get me to attend this thing called a Women's Weekend. Her husband started it by going into the woods during a Men's Weekend where he beat a drum while dancing naked around a fire and chanting like a warrior about his manhood—or something like that. And apparently he wanted a warrior wife, too. So, she obeyed and from that point claimed her "marriage had never been better." Well, I already thought I had a good marriage and didn't need or want to dance naked in front of anyone other than my husband. But as our friendship developed, I admit I grew more curious about this weekend C.L. so desperately wanted me to experience. When I finally ran out of legitimate excuses, I signed up to please her. For the sake of our friendship I agreed to participate in an expensive program I knew nothing about other than that it was supposed to bring us closer and do wonders for all my relationships.

I soon learned that the weekend was a plunge into a caldron bubbling over with well-orchestrated pshycobabble designed to get me to join a tribe of Stepford Wives—the robotic husband-pleasers in a 1970s made-for-TV movie. The process intended to break us into a thousand pieces on

The Things I Wish I'd Said

Saturday and then glue our Humpty-Dumpty shards back together forty-eight hours later. There were no guarantees, of course, and I signed a waiver guarding my hosts against potential physical, emotional and mental injuries without limitation I might endure as a result of the weekend. As C.L. begged me to participate and she was still pretty "normal," I trusted her and therefore subjected myself to a weekend of torture techniques such as sleep and food deprivation, authoritarian conditions including bright lights and guards at every exit denying me the opportunity to use the restroom. Droning, repetitive material boomed over a loud speaker in a voice like the Wizard of Oz (when he was still the man behind the curtain), and they allowed virtually no opportunity for questions or feedback.

Can you say, "mind control?"

A spin off of EST (Erhart's Seminary Training)—itself an offshoot of the 1970s Human Potential Movement—I'd have to dig deep to remember the name of the organization hosting the event since I purposefully suppressed the memory. So, for the sake of cult-free-thinking and my over-taxed mommy brain, I'll just refer to it as The Stepford Foundation.

The Stepford Foundation was a post university sorority that hosted a series of rush parties for anyone willing to pay the fees; but as was evident at the one rush party I attended during my freshman year of college (because of the free beer), they had a slate of personality and behavior requirements of their ultimate membership. Back when I walked in the door and into that rush party, the ranking officers took one look at the long hippie hair on my friend Carol and me and blatantly shook their heads, "no," and pointed towards the keg in the corner of the room. As we each sipped on a plastic cup filled with foam that smelled like beer and tasted like nothing, no one talked to us. Sufficiently and successfully snubbed, we hightailed it out of there and never looked back at the Greek section of campus.

With the Stepford Foundation it wasn't my looks that made me undesirable at first glance. It was my occupation as a newspaper columnist. When the Foundation learned I worked for a newspaper, the mute, robotic paper-pushers paid particular attention to my oath of silence and required that I sign an additional stack of paranoia forms before I agreed to participate.

I had already paid my money, (was it four hundred dollars? Six hundred? I can't remember), and assumed it was a non-refundable fee. And since I had waltzed through the iron doors with an I'm-ready-for-anything-attitude, I agreed to strap on the chastity belt of confidentiality. Eventually I understood their reasons for coveting confidentiality because the Foundation depended on their newly armored women warriors to go out and recruit others to pay steep fees and share in this metamorphosis of a weekend experience.

The weekend kicked off with an hour or so of pseudo silence where we sat on the floor in a hallway of what felt like a cross between a church and a prison. It reminded me of waiting for concert tickets in the days where waiting in line for groups like the Talking Heads, The Grateful Dead or Bruce Springsteen was my idea of a party. No one really wanted to be in that cold, uncomfortable place so early in the morning, but because of the reward waiting at the ticket window and the looks on your friends faces when you announce that you scored ten front row seats, the air was filled with the promise of a pending carnival. But we sat too long. And no one really knew what waited for us inside the arena.

Finally, we filtered into a large ballroom where two or three hundred cold metal chairs were positioned in rows and facing a stage lined with swooping velvet curtains. Slowly and robotically filing into formation—the opposite of the pandemonium concert crowds experience when the flood gates open at venues with stadium seating, where rabid fans race to reserve the best seats in the house—the group of tired women with searching eyes was soon seated delicate shoulder to delicate shoulder and crossed leg to crossed leg.

And there we sat. And sat. And sat.

Many wondered if we had just paid to sit in a room for two days with a bunch of clueless women. Finally, one of the more extroverted women moseyed up to the stage and took hold of the microphone. "My name is Nancy," she said. "And I don't know what I'm doing here, but I thought I'd just get up to say hi to all of you."

The Things I Wish I'd Said

Thus began a barrage of introductions.

"I'm Sheila and my friend made me do this. She told me to have faith."

"I'm Tiffany and I flew all the way in from Massachusetts for this seminar, so it better be good."

"I'm not going to say my name because I think this whole thing is a crock of shit. I paid good money to come here and do what? Sit in a room all day with the likes of you people?"

"My name is Gwendolyn and most people I know hate me because I'm beautiful. I'm here to find out why."

Oh-kay, I thought. *That* was different. And at once Gwendolyn spun on a high-heeled shoe and her thick strawberry blonde mane swung around one shoulder like a shampoo commercial. A collective groan arose from the audience.

After Gwendolyn the Beautiful handed over the microphone, the speakers grew louder and more obnoxious. It was as though she had granted permission to really say something.

"Gwendolyn baby, you ain't so hot," said one.

"Well, I think you *are* beautiful, Gwendolyn," said another. "But so am I. And so are all of you. We're women and we're all beautiful. That's why we're here, right?"

Many yelled into the microphone—hissing and popping—that they were hungry and wanted to eat. Others were irate over the militant and mute warriors guarding the doors, who refused to let anyone out to pee or get a drink of water.

And then the droning began. If my life depended on it, I couldn't repeat what this booming voice said over a loud speaker. It might have called us "jerks," or even "assholes." Contrary to what several of our fellow weekenders told us from the stage just prior to the droning, I think our booming voice said we were stupid and even ugly.

When the droning man behind the loudspeaker finally entered the room, he roamed the aisles with a microphone as if he were Phil Donahue and kept right on droning. In fact, a camera followed his every move and he humiliated anyone who dared to speak or ask a question. Remember the encouraging statement teachers once gave at the beginning of the school year when "no question was a dumb question?" Well, this was the beginning of a weekend meant to undo everything we had been taught. Challenging questions were products of ego and the Donahue character's main message was that ego had no place in the personality of a woman.

As the weekend experience seeped through my pores, I wondered how this rather unattractive, loudmouth and misogynistic person intended to turn me into more-than-a woman. He claimed to know thousands of women and said he'd heard it all. He also proclaimed to be happily married with a gorgeous, Stepford trophy wife at home.

I stuck with the weekend until the bitter end—gaining some insight in some areas and dismissing other information as unhelpful—and walked out forty-eight hours later a successful woman warrior, singing the Helen Ready anthem "I Am Woman." I learned a lot about my fear of anger and confirmed my love of humor and ultimately, I shared a lot of laughs with some pretty hilarious and yes, beautiful women.

C.L. was at my candlelit graduation ceremony with flowers and kisses and well wishes and I had made her very happy. I made her happy because she finally got her team of Stepford warriors off her back, who prior to her success in getting me to sign up, accused her of not taking proper care of her relationships.

The weekend brought us closer for a little while and if memory serves, it was after this experience that I wrote the above column. I even tried to join a warrior team. But the foul taste I experienced from the beginning grew overwhelming. Things were going too well in my life to join this cult. And on the afternoon I saw the droning man himself spreading his sound bite philosophy on a national TV talk show, I knew I had been duped. Part of the confidentiality clause indicated that any part of the weekend taken out of context would be misunderstood by the masses and cause harm to the Foundation's purpose. And yet there he was spouting little sections of the weekend in-between commercials for personal hygiene products and adjustable beds.

C.L. didn't seem to mind that I abandoned the program. She had gotten what she wanted, and since we were allowed to talk to other "graduates" about our experiences, it enabled her to open up to me a whole lot more. But frankly, she opened up too much and this is when I pulled away.

Simply put, I think there are some areas that really should remain private—even between the best of friends. I, for example, wasn't the least bit interested in the details of her or anyone's sex life—domestic *or* extracurricular. And since the weekend, all she wanted to talk about was domestic sex—in other words, what went on between her husband and her in the bedroom. Ugh!

Sex and the City may be a hot topic of conversation for singles in search of the perfect relationship, but Sex and the Suburbs just isn't the same. Not even in California.

An Inch Off the Bottom

November 15, 1992

Ever since the day the stylist at Andy's Unisex Barber Shop said the words, "Let me do something wonderful with your hair" I've had a deadly fear of getting my hair cut.

I was a typically trendy teenager, anxious to become a member of the Farrah Fawcett-Jones hairstyle club. We all wanted hair like Farrah, and my hair had the potential. It was long and thick with lots of natural curl. It had a variety of colors, different hues of brown, red and blonde, all mixed together. Never mind that I had as many zits as freckles on my face and a mouth full of braces. I had great hair. And the stylist at Andy's was the first of a long string of one-haircut-stand beauticians to tell me so.

I remember sitting in her soft leather chair, watching in the mirror as she draped a giant plastic bib around my neck. A woman in the chair next to me was flipping frantically through magazines, complaining that none of the styles was right for her. "Everything looks too young," she said. "Not everyone wants to look like one of Charlie's Angels!"

I couldn't believe the coincidence.

"So, what do you have in mind?" asked the stylist while she combed through my hair with her fingers. I could feel her long, sharp nails massaging my scalp and was tempted to ask her just to scratch my head for a while.

"Can you layer it a little?" I asked. (There was no way I was going to mention the name "Farrah" with this frustrated woman next to me still tearing through magazines.)

89

The Things I Wish I'd Said

"Are you sure you want to go with layers?" she asked.

"I'm sure," I said, certain that I needed a new look to make up for the rest of me. And then the stylist said THE WORDS: "Why don't you let me do something wonderful with your hair?"

I had no idea that these words would soon become my personal Pavlovian prompter to say, "See you later," find a brush and a rubber band, and organize my own follicles into a tight, tight braid. Since I was trusting (and stupid), I nodded vigorously, excited about the possibility of being transformed into "something wonderful."

The stylist then washed and conditioned my hair with stuff that smelled like strawberry incense. Then back to the leather chair. She flipped on a couple of heat lamps, declaring that the ultra-violet light was the latest trend in styling. The light rays, she claimed, enabled her to see the natural waves of my hair.

I was impressed.

I can't remember how long the whole process took, but I do remember imagining locks of my hair hitting the tile. They lay there looking like the thick, slimy worms we had recently dissected in biology class. Suddenly I realized there was an awful lot of hair piling up on the floor.

"Are you almost done?" I asked, attempting to mask my escalating alarm. The sound of snipping scissors was beginning to sound like fingernails on a chalkboard. I wanted her to stop cutting.

"Almost," she said. "I just need to blow-dry and style a bit, and then we'll have a whole new you."

As I looked into the mirror at the wet stringy mop on top of my head, I wondered if my mother would recognize the "new me." I didn't even recognize myself. Thanks to this snip-happy stylist, my beautiful hair looked like sauceless spaghetti.

I avoided the mirror through the blow-dry and also while she used a whiskbroom to brush away the stray hairs from my face and neck. When the stylist had finally finished what she considered a masterpiece, I timidly opened my eyes. Did I look like Farrah Fawcett? No way. I looked more like Annette Funicello in a Mickey Mouse hat. All my beloved blonde streaks had disappeared. I'd never seen my hair so dark. It hung just above my shoulders. The top was layered, but the layers were so short that the hairs stuck straight up on top and straight out at my temples. I looked like I'd just gotten out of bed after a lousy night's sleep.

I felt like crying, like I wanted to get under the covers and not come out until my hair grew back.

"Well?" chirped the stylist. "What do you think?"

Before I could choke out a response, I heard someone ask, "Can you do that to my hair?"

It was the lady next to me.

I'm Worth It

My editor had a huge hand in styling the "Inch Off The Bottom" piece. She, for example, came up with "sauceless spaghetti," replacing my word, "noodles." Noodles happen to be my kids' favorite meal. If I sat them down and asked if they wanted "sauceless spaghetti" for dinner, they'd surely screw up their faces and ask me if I was trying to serve them a science experiment. My current word processing program keeps offering a squiggly red underline beneath the word "sauceless." Ooh! There it is again. The animated little icon winking and nodding at me in the upper right hand corner of my computer would prefer it if I used the word "sauciness" or separated this non-word into "sauce" and "less." I guess columnists are sometimes given license to make up words. I even made up part of this story. The bad haircut—the Mullet—actually happened, but the lady in the chair came from a conglomerate of characters seated next to me in salons across America.

These days I no longer go to a salon to have my hair reinterpreted. Instead, I go to the private studio of a neighbor, who happens to be the most fabulous stylist I've ever had. And I am completely at his mercy. His name is Tommy and as far as I'm concerned, what he says, goes.

Tommy is this aging hippy's hero. Bless his heart, he *won't* let me have short hair. Even when I request an inch off the bottom, he's more likely to take off half that. And layers? Bite your tongue. While layered hair is still sported in places like malls around the country, to me it's as dead and buried as the 1970s.

As a result of the stylist's creation on my teen-aged head that I like to call "A Disaster in Layers," I spent my entire college career looking like something along the lines of Cousin Itt. My hair grew long. Really long. During my freshman year, the black girls in my dorm taught me how to make corn-rows (the white girls called it French braiding) and my long fingers took to this task like a senior looking for blow-off credits takes to an underwater basket weaving course. I became so good at it that many of the other long-hairs lined up outside my bathroom door for morning "follicle organizing." The problems were that I'd run out of time to braid my own hair, or by the time I got to the ends of my long strands, my hands were tired. As a result I developed the habit of twisting my ponytail into a rope and tying it into a knot. (My hair is in a knot at this moment.) And while I don't carry around all the length I sported as a co-ed, I'm a forty-something mother these days after all, I have one rule about the length of my hair. It's got to be long enough to tie in a knot. If I didn't have the opportunity to tie and retie my hair all day long, it would be as traumatic as not having the ability to brush my teeth four or five times a day.

I was born with red hair. Since most of my baby pictures are in black and white and my hair didn't stay red, I have to take my mother's word on this. Most of my baby pictures paint me as a blonde—at least in the summer—but in the winter, pigment definitely came into play. And as I got older, my hair got darker.

What's up with that anyway? When I met my husband over twenty years ago, he could only be described as a blond. But today, underneath the gray his hair is dark brown. The first child we produced together, Willow, has hair so white she's often called "Blondie," by well-meaning passersby. They look at her and then look at us and ask: "Where does she get the blonde hair?" I want to answer "the UPS man"—as opposed to using the old milkman line, because I haven't seen a milkman pull up to my door since 1968, when Mr. Martin, who lived across the street and drove the Berwyn Dairy truck left his box of Bazooka bubblegum out for us to steal. But I always point to her daddy and say that he had the same towhead for the first half of his life. All of our nieces and nephews on his side have light hair and I've noticed that the older kids are fading into colors that will eventually require them to change their personal descriptions on their driver's licenses. Luckily the girls who don't want to give up monikers like "Blondie," have the option of "highlights."

After taking charge of my length, I, like many blonde-wannabe girls, ventured into the world of color. Shortly before our wedding, I went to a salon to "get some streaks" put into my hair. And it turned out that I chose the right salon on the right day because they were in the process of setting up a show. I didn't know what they meant when they asked me to be a model, but I was delighted to get a color process for free. As long as my hair stayed long enough to tie into a knot, I figured, how bad could it be?

On the day of the show I arrived at the designated time and sat in my assigned chair. Things were going on all around me, but I buried my nose in the salon bible (*People* magazine) and didn't pay much attention. But my turn finally came.

"Okay are you ready?" boomed a voice from behind me just as my chair was spun to face the mirror. "I'm your colorist and you're next."

I looked into the mirror, only to see a horrific image hovering over my unsuspecting head. My so-called colorist, the woman I was about to trust with the job of coloring my hair before my wedding, looked like an enormous, chartreuse rooster. Her haircut is known as a "spike," and I can't bring myself to say it was in style at that punk-point in 1980s history. How anyone might consider this look the least bit attractive is beyond my comprehension. Underneath the chartreuse tips of her statue-of-liberty type crown nudged muddy black roots, while black stipple dots encompassed the rest of her head. It was a five-o'clock shadow in the northern hemisphere of her skull. And it gets worse.

She wore black-rimmed, Elvis Costello glasses and bright red lipstick. And she was a large woman, with big hands and a strong voice. It was like a cartoon character had come to life and it wielded both scissors and chemicals! Each of my petrified internal instincts screamed at me to run, however, I didn't think I could escape the strong clutches of the chartreuse rooster.

The Things I Wish I'd Said

"Is my hair going to come out similar in color to yours?" I finally managed.

"No, dear," she laughed. "This is more like the Crayola-crayon line. Today we're demonstrating a more sophisticated line. We're going to weave together two of your natural colors into the darker areas and it's going to be wonderful. Trust me."

Wonderful. There was that word again. The chartreuse rooster was going to do something wonderful with my hair. I spent the entire session with my eyes squeezed shut. And in spite of my apprehension and the five pounds I lost while sweating it out in her chair, it *was* wonderful. (And I've got the wedding pictures to prove it.) So, I guess it's fair to say that my faith in hair stylists—or at least in colorists—was renewed.

When moving to a new town, there are three things that every woman needs: A gynecologist, a dentist and a hairdresser. My neighbors were responsible for helping me find all three. Turns out, save one, every woman and teenage girl on our little corner of the neighborhood we like to call "The Center of the Universe," has a regular date with Tommy the wonder-stylist. "Is Tommy *doing* you this evening?" we sometimes ask. Or if someone is looking particularly stylish at the bus stop one morning we'll say, "Oh, you've been to see Tommy, haven't you?" And then we'll fine her a quarter for looking so nice before the rest of us have had a chance to even comb our hair before getting our kids out the door.

Some women may pooh-pooh the need for a hairdresser as they grab their Clairol and Loreal boxes off the shelves at Osco and Walgreens and battle the gray every few weeks; however, there's nothing like the experience of having the perfect stylist care about your most distinctive feature and massage your scalp with a luxurious shampoo. Each time I spend an evening in Tommy's studio, I lay out the cash, kiss him on the cheek and say, "I'm worth it."

So are you.

Deadhead Withdrawal

I had to look back into an old journal to begin this column because I wasn't sure exactly when it was that I first considered myself to be a Deadhead. (Translation for those who are totally out of the music scene: Grateful Dead groupie). It happened during three shows at Berkeley's Greek Theater in 1983 on a weekend beginning with a Friday the Thirteenth.

For the record, these shows were not the first I attended. I was familiar with the Deadhead scene during college due to Deadhead roommate after Deadhead roommate. At that time, although I liked the music, I hadn't yet grasped the physical, mental and, like, total take-over peaceful transformation that happened to me once I experienced this phenomenon, this band called The Grateful Dead, in the Golden State.

"A new consciousness emerged within me," my journal reads. "We were with all our friends. Things were so light and carefree but then the music made everything so intense. The people became so beautiful to me.

"The Dead played 'Morning Dew' and 'China Doll' and we all held hands and hugged and I cried so hard. I had never felt more wonderful in my life thinking how lucky we all were to be there and enjoying ourselves so much. The people were so bizarre, so happy and full of life, music and peace. You could be as weird and wild as you wanted and it didn't bother anyone."

The journal passage goes on describing the party that never seemed to end. As long as the music continued and the people were free and, like the song goes, "Dancin' in the Streets," I was happy to just be a part of it.

The Things I Wish I'd Said

•••

This began several new, long-term friendships and about a five year invest-ment of time, tapes and concert tickets that seemed to go up in price with every show. I lost count after the 100th show, but I can still count the num-ber of states in which I've seen the Dead perform: Five. The highest eleva-tion: Boreal Ridge. The lowest elevation: Ventura Beach.

I was a Deadhead and proud of it. If a show was coming up, I knew about it and most likely had a ticket. It was very rare for me to be one of those lost souls out front amidst the traveling carnival and boutique saying to passersby, "I need a miracle" (i.e. I need a ticket to the show.)

Things are different now.

Today I am a recovering Deadhead. I realized this last weekend when I turned down tickets to see the Grateful Dead at the Shoreline Amphithe-ater. In fact, I haven't seen the band since last New Year's Eve at the Oak-land Coliseum and have no plans to seem them play in the near future.

While a "Steal Your Face" sticker (the Deadhead emblem, which might compare to the Good Sam Club stickers seen on Winnebagos) is still on my car and a colorful collection of tie-dyed shirts lines the bottom of my dresser drawer, it has gotten to the point where I cringe whenever I hear a scratchy concert tape wail out from anybody's tape deck. It reminds me of the time years ago when some friends and I threw Partridge Family albums against the fireplace because we had heard "I Think I Love You" just a few too many times.

In this case I've heard what I thought was the Dead's endless repertoire played too many times. I've watched Bobby Weir turn into a screaming rock star, Jerry Garcia into a white-haired, overweight junkie. And key-board players seem to disappear one after the other like the spontaneously combusting band members in the movie "This is Spinal Tap."

As I grow older I've seen the Deadheads get younger. I've seen too many bare feet and drug overdoses, and too much public urination. I've seen community outrage at the traveling band of Gypsies and their sepul-chral buses and hence the cancellation of shows at my favorite places like

Berkeley's Greek Theater, Henry J. Kaiser Convention Center and Stanford's Frost Amphitheater. I've seen Bill Graham become very rich and while I admire the various benefits he sponsors and for that matter, the Dead's contributions to save the rain forests, the whole thing has become too much of a mercantile mire for me.

I guess it was all a phase.

Turning back to my journal, I referred to "the Deadhead Highway," or what I called the parade of people leaving the show and wrote: "We strolled through the pathways looking at everybody and being looked at by everybody else. Everyone was so pretty, gorgeous even . . . turned on and getting so much out of life and from one another. I hope things don't change."

As I experience my withdrawal, I wonder. Did things change or did I?

Dead End

"You stopped doing drugs." That's what a little note on the bottom of my submission read, courtesy of my copyeditor.

Yes, I suppose I did stop doing drugs. You have to stop eventually or you die. And now that Jerry Garcia is dead and buried, a lot of other people have probably stopped, too. Jerry, a perennial heroine user, died in a drug rehab treatment center in Forest Knolls, California in August of 1995. And as much as I was deeply saddened by his passing, perhaps it was a fitting end to his long, strange trip on this planet. Life for all of us eventually must come to a dead end.

So, what was it like to be a Deadhead? Allow me a little flashback time.

Learning about the Deadhead chapter in my history is a mere amusement for most of my adult friends. These are friends with whom I now attend fund-raising events for our kids' schools and pageant rehearsals at our church. "We figured you were a former hippie because of the long hair," they say. "But a Deadhead?!"

"Former-*schmormer*," I scoff. "Once a hippie, always a hippie. There's nothing former about me."

I'll bet you can still pick me out of the SUV-driving, church going and fund-raising set. I may wear pearls, but I'm wearing them with blue jeans and at any given time I pull out the French twist neatly gathered at the back of my head and organize my hair into braids. I still have my Birkenstocks, even though now I think they're pretty ugly too, and my little girls look darn cute in the tie-dyed dresses we pick up at the Fourth Avenue Street Fairs in Tucson twice a year.

Once you've been dipped in the colorful tie-dyed world of the Grateful Dead, it leaves permanent rainbows on your skin. It's like a tattoo. And while I consider my clothing to be perfectly normal, the two words that often describe me (besides tall and skinny) are "funky" and "artistic." And this is not always meant as a compliment. I see it in the condescending eyes of the commentator. We hippies have eyes in the backs of our heads and will always insist that the intake of mind-altering substances gave us an expanded vision of the world. How else can you explain the ability to see wooden doors breathe and hear amethyst crystals scream out harmonic tones?

I've noticed that because of my years in the funky world of the Grateful Dead, sometimes I'm not taken seriously. People who are unfamiliar with the Grateful Dead and think their unique combination of rock-and-roll and folk music might instead be unholy, cryptic or on a par with "acid rock," assume that "deadhead" is synonymous with "empty headedness." (Either that or it's something they do to the flowering plants in their gardens each summer.) Even though this label is totally unjustified, since I am not even remotely empty headed, I understand it. It's on a par with how I feel about kids with pierced noses.

Whenever I have a conversation with someone who has a pierced nose, I find myself staring at the nose hole above the nose hole and not really listening to what she's saying. And this is especially true if she sports a ring rather than a stud. I can't help but think it looks like a leech that is sucking the life (and the boogers) out of her nose. If either of my daughters ever asks permission to have her nose pierced I will respond by saying, "if you ever want anyone to take you seriously again, *don't* do it." I hope that works; however, I realize that neither one is likely to ask me for permission to pierce anything. I pierced my own ears on the sly when I was in sixth grade, and my father raised holy stink when he found out. He equated pierced ears with hookers—or something like that. He punished me by never letting me take the car once I had my driver's license.

"Dad, can I borrow the car to go to the mall?"

"No. You have holes in your ears, you little slut!"

The people who care the most about what it meant to be a Deadhead are kids in their early twenties who wear tie-dyed shirts and have cars full of bumper stickers with dancing bears and statements like "Imagine Whirled Peas." (Many of them have pierced noses, too.) They go off in their "vintage" Volkswagen buses on Phish junkets or listen to the Colorado bluegrass band, String Cheese Incident, trying to get a taste of the Deadhead life and be hippies in twenty-first century society. A society where music is synthesized, digitized and packaged in half-dressed, anorexic frames wiggling away on MTV. The century may have changed but the age has not. Youthful angst is the need to either protest something or break out of the conservative normalcy facing them in the adult world.

If you weren't a Deadhead in the 1980s during the height of the Grateful Dead's popularity, chances are you didn't know they put on shows after the days of Haight-Ashbury. And you didn't know that Deadheads were not all just acid or mushroom dropping, dreadlock wearing, smelly, bell-clad gypsies. We Deadheads came from all walks. We were lawyers and engineers, teachers, doctors, stockbrokers and journalists. Some of us were accountants, others were truck drivers. Many of us owned homes and businesses. We had children named Cassidy and dogs named Stella Blue. And we were one, big happy family. In news articles about his death, the mainstream media titled Jerry a "1960s icon." But his real popularity, his true following, soared in the 1980s.

I know where I was and what I was doing on the August day of 1995 when Jerry Garcia died, the same way I know where I was when I heard about John Lennon's murder and where my mother told me I was when President Kennedy was shot. (Since I was only three, I can't recall hearing the news, but my mother told me I was in front of the television watching

Bozo the Clown when her friend called.) As for Lennon, I was driving home in my '63 Dodge Dart after buying a Christmas tree with my boyfriend when the shocking news came over the radio. As a broke college student I remember decorating that anorexic Charlie Brown tree with homemade and improvised ornaments including a bottle of "Liquid Paper" with a red ribbon tied to it. I still have that ornament, although the paper inside is no longer liquid and it sounds like a maraca filled with rice kernels when you shake it. But the red ribbon is in tact and each year when it decorates our Christmas tree, I think of John Lennon and mourn the loss.

The day we heard Jerry died, we spent a lot of time on the phone. Our Deadhead friends called from across the country and through our conversations, as Jerry's unmistakable guitar filled the room, we reminisced about the hundreds of shows we all attended together.

"I remember how you were the first person I ran into at each show," I told my friend OD. "You never failed to greet me with the smile of a Cheshire cat and a warm hug."

"My most memorable Dead show was the time I saw a guy slit his own throat in Ventura," said my husband.

"I got stung by a bee in Ventura at a show while walking across a grass field in my bare feet," I said. "I was twenty-five and it was my first bee sting."

"Remember my first show when you picked me up from the airport and said you were taking me some place special?" asked my sister Gayle. "I thought you were taking me to a basketball game, but when I ended up at a Dead show I was thrilled. I remember playing volleyball at the Henry J. Kaiser auditorium in Oakland. I couldn't believe we played volleyball at a concert!"

"I loved the time you and Mike were dressed as Elvis and Pricilla at a Halloween Show," said my friend Ricky. "I thought Mike looked more like a game show host and that you were Vanna White. You kept asking me if I wanted to buy a vowel."

"One time at the Greek Theater in Berkeley I found myself next to Allison the hair-dancer and I quickly darted in another direction. She usually stood between the hair-dancers known as "Cousin Itt" and "The Other One," and with her high-pitched scream and chest-massaging dancing, I didn't want anyone to think I was 'one of them,'" said another friend.

"At one show at the Greek Theater I was hanging out by the stage before the show and Jerry walked right passed me," I said. "He looked at me and I simply said, 'hey Jerry,' and he said 'hey' right back to me."

Jerry Garcia, perhaps best known for his guitar playing, could make me cry when he sang. Some days he was not in the best voice, but on the days when he was, he crooned a reedy ballad, and I'm not kidding, the eucalyptus trees surrounding the outdoor theaters of the Cal Greek Theater or Stanford Frost Amphitheater swayed in response. And this isn't drugs talking. This is talent. A talent so rich, so natural and so unique, it kept thousands of us coming back again and again to make it the backdrop of our family gatherings.

Yes, it was a long, strange trip, but in the end, I'm grateful for the memories.

What's in a name? It's MINE. That's what.

July 30, 1991

Did you hear about the woman in Salt Lake City who was required to get her ex-husband's permission in order to change the name on her driver's license back to the name with which she was born?

According to Utah law, name changes are allowed at the time of divorce, which in this case was in 1988. The Utah Driver License Division specifies that a woman cannot unilaterally change her name after the divorce without an amendment to the divorce decree. They say this is a guard against fraud and not, as the woman and her lawyer charged, a practice of sexual discrimination against divorced women.

A Utah court and a federal appeals court have rejected her claim.

Twenty years ago it wasn't a common practice among women to keep their maiden names after marriage. Unless you were a movie star or celebrity of some sort, it probably wasn't discussed. Marriage vows insinuated that you would love, honor and agree to be called by a different name than the one to which you had answered all your life.

These days, however, I know more women around my age who have decided not to take their husband's names than those who have.

"Are you keeping your name?" has become a common question asked at bridal showers and rehearsal dinners. And it is important that the bride-to-be has an immediate answer. If you're wishy-washy on the subject like I was, there are those (like parents, relatives and married friends who dis-

103

carded their own names without thought) who will immediately begin sending you letters addressed to a name that makes you feel as though you are opening someone else's mail. Even when you inform them that you have not changed your name, the mail keeps coming with the new, married name. (Sometimes they have the courtesy to hyphenate the old and new last names.)

I've been married for nearly two years and it has gotten to the point where I don't know what my name is anymore.

Because my maiden name begins with a V, the only benefit I ever saw in a name change was perhaps getting closer to the beginning of the alphabet. But that didn't seem like such a bonus once I got out of school and away from roll calls and jump rope lines arranged by ABC's.

It's not that I don't like my husband's family name. It's a great name—and it's at the beginning of the alphabet. The truth is that I do use it and even answer to it once in a while for the sake of convenience. But officially, I'm still a VanOrt. That's the name on my driver's license.

I gave the decision a lot of thought. How, I asked myself, could I give up my name? It's the only thing unique about me. And when I finally made up my mind to keep it, I had the support of my husband. I believe his exact words were: "I'd be flattered if you took my name; but I don't mind that you decided not to."

My ultimate reasoning was simple. I had just made it through my twenties—the identity years, as they're called. I felt I couldn't afford to take on an identity crisis after such a funky decade and a name change might just have triggered such an event.

But it seems my deliberation was for naught. It's not like I have some judicial system breathing down my neck like the woman in Utah; but I live in a society that still looks at you like you're a little weird when you keep your maiden name.

In Switzerland, men and women adopt each other's family names at marriage—combining them in hyphenation. It seems like such a practical way of handling this name thing. And for a country that only recently gave women the right to vote and still won't allow its citizens to work on Sundays, that's pretty progressive family planning.

Yet according to my friend, Robin, who married a Swiss man and now lives with him and their two children in the idyllic, orderly Swiss hills, tradition states that the man's name goes first. She would have no part of that and in defiance of her neighbors and in-laws; her name is on the front end of the hyphen.

Some people are never satisfied.

Long ago William Shakespeare wrote Juliet's poetic words: *"What's in a name? That which we call a rose/By any other name would smell as sweet."*

He had a good point. The way I see it is that my friend in Switzerland, regardless of names and hyphens, will always be simply "Robin" to me. And to her, well, she still calls me "Ort."

I Married 'My Cousin'

The first time I wrote a letter to the man who is now my husband I spelled his last name wrong. Who wouldn't think "c-o-u-s-i-n-s" *isn't* the way to spell a name pronounced the same way you pronounce what your aunt's kids are called? I was shocked when he returned my letter, primarily because he returned my letter and secondly because the return address showed his name was not Cousins, but rather, Cozzens.

Since taking his name when we went into business together, I officially changed my middle name to VanOrt and my last name to Cozzens. No hyphen, just three names. We gave our children this last name as well and I've seen it misspelled and mispronounced (with a long 'o') hundreds of times. And while I've gotten used to it, our second grader is only beginning to know the feeling of going through life with an unusual name. She thought it was funny when her class photo came home with the name "Willow Cousins" under her smiling face. I assured her it wouldn't be the last time she faced such an error. Since she's the only Willow in the school, and probably the county, she could probably just go by her first name and not even worry about whether or not her last name is spelled correctly.

I've spent my entire life seeing my name misspelled. It's what happens when you have an unconventional spelling. I know five people who constantly refer to me as "Michele with one L" instead of just Michele. (Anne with an e, you're one of them.) And each time someone asks me if I have "one L or two?" I know they either share my first name or have a Michele (or Michelle) in their life. In spite of my lifelong disdain for a double L in my name, both my daughters have names with a double L: Willow and Camille. And in Camille's case, even her middle name has a double L: Ellen.

But for as many times as my names have been misspelled over the years, nothing beats seeing jaws drop when people think I say I married "my cousin." This is because my wonderful husband's name is Mike. Glide over "Mike" too quickly and it can sound like "my."

Whenever someone thinks they heard me say I married my cousin, I usually respond by saying something like, "Yep, marryin' my cousin was just about the dern smartest thing I ever done."

And I'm proud to have his name.

Resolution Redux

January 7, 1992

Superstitions and resolutions have never been high on my list of priorities. They do fascinate me, however. Especially at this time of year when we tend to whitewash our personalities and reshape our figures.

Losing weight probably tops the United States resolution list again this year. It has been the resolution of the decade—the resolution of modern times.

I'm not sure what organization compiles the list of most popular resolutions but it's probably related to some women's magazine or any vehicle used for Jenny Craig and Nutri/system advertisements. Weight loss center and health club memberships soar every January as a result of this resolution. While retail centers depend on Christmas for annual revenue, fat farms need January.

I joined a health club one January a few years back. I didn't join to lose weight necessarily. I joined to gain muscles. But I dropped out of biceps development classes sometime around late spring when the weather got warm and the workout room got smelly. I prefer to get my exercise out of doors.

My resolutions are more like passing thoughts. For example, every year I'd like to be nicer. I'd like to file all my paperwork on a regular basis. I'd like to set up a budget and stick to it. I'd like to read more books and watch less television.

Ever since I got out of school I guess I stopped being goal oriented. And what good are resolutions without goals?

107

The Things I Wish I'd Said

• • •

Superstitions, on the other hand, are more in line with the passing thought philosophy. Sure they trigger actions. But superstitions have nothing to do with goals.

When I was a Girl Scout there were a variety of superstitions bequeathed to me from the older girls. They came out during bus rides to overnight camp. I remember we had to hold up our feet every time the bus rode over railroad tracks. It meant bad luck if we didn't—torrential rain through leaky tents or spiders in our sleeping bags.

And every time we saw an ambulance or funeral procession, we had to "hold a button." This means to put your fingers around a button on a jacket, a shirt or the one above the zipper on your pants. Failure to do so meant illness or death in your immediate future.

We had the popular "step on a crack, break your mother's back," as we walked the sidewalk paths to school, and the well-known fear of a black cat crossing in front of us. We never walked under ladders and were extra cautious on Friday the Thirteenth. My younger sister was born on a Friday the Thirteenth, so she always acted like she owned the day whenever it came around. On any Friday the Thirteenth, I figured if I hung around with her, I didn't have to be as wary.

A new superstition that crossed my path a few years back was taught to me by a former coworker named Cate. Cate learned from her granny that on the first day of every month, if the first words you uttered were "rabbit, rabbit, rabbit," you'd have good luck for the rest of the month.

Over the holidays I spoke with my husband's aunt who had recently heard the same superstition with a couple variations. Her version is that you should say "rabbit, rabbit" (the word twice instead of three times) and on the first day of the year for good luck in the new year. It was definitely the more conservation version.

Then I learned about a holiday good luck superstition that takes place on Christmas Eve day. It goes like this: When you wake up on December 24 and the first person you see is a man, you'll have good luck for the new year to come. If you see a woman first, you'll have bad luck.

I wonder how many single women subscribing to this superstition avoid the mirror before they go out on the day before Christmas. Lesbians are in deep trouble with this one. As for gay men, well I guess they have it made.

The first person I saw on December 24 was my unhappy husband who was sleeping next to me in the fold out bed at my sister's house. So I'll have good luck. He, on the other hand, saw me.

The next thing we heard was the loud "meow" of my sister's cat. He's allergic to cats. Then he went to take a shower and the pilot light of the water heater had extinguished during the night and there was no hot water.

It's going to be a long year.

Multiple Rabbits

My daughter never misses the opportunity to say "rabbit, rabbit, rabbit" on the first day of the month. I told her this story when she was five and she has kept track of the calendar ever since. I don't think she does it for good luck, per se, since I'm not sure she comprehends the concepts of good and bad luck. For her it's a game and she likes to play it.

While my older daughter this year resolved to finish reading the *Babysitter's Club* series, I'm quite sure my youngest has never formulated a New Year's resolution. I figure kids first should be old enough to make it to the stroke of midnight on New Year's Eve before they vow to make their beds, pick up their rooms and put their dirty dishes in the dishwasher for the next three-hundred, sixty-five days. And I have yet to share the phenomenon known as Friday the Thirteenth with them, although the first time one comes home from school and says it's a "bad luck day," I will immediately set her straight.

In the year the above column ran, 1992, there were two Friday the Thirteenths. And the newspaper's feature editor thought we should do a story on the history of that day. Just my luck, I was the chosen writer. But it turned out to be a fun and enlightening assignment. While researching, I haunted the metaphysical bookstores dotting the San Francisco Bay area and had the unique opportunity to talk to witches. Yes, actual witches. They had witchy names like Sitara and Alba (making me think of Samantha and Tabitha), and they insisted that Friday the Thirteenth was the luckiest day of the year. I knew going in the door that the traditional number for a coven of witches is thirteen, but Sitara and Alba taught me so much more.

"Friday is the sacred day of the Norse Goddess Freya, making it a lucky day," said Sitara. "And in the times of pagan religions, when the female was divine, the number thirteen was revered. It was drawn from the thirteen months of the lunar (and menstrual) calendar."

Alba, a high priestess said that Friday the Thirteenth got its bad name from Christian monks. "Throughout history when one religion takes over another, the old gods become the new demons," she said. "Prior to Christianity, most cultures worshipped the Goddess. Therefore (when Christianity emerged), everything associated with pagan female divinity was called unlucky."

By reading the books they suggested (and happily sold to me), I learned that Christianity was indeed most likely responsible for spreading the fear of Friday the Thirteenth. For example, it is believed that Christ was crucified on a Friday and as a result, Fridays became a day of fasting, fish-eating and gloom. Friday also became known as "hangman's day" in many countries, a day on which criminals were executed. As for thirteen, the Christian church opposed all pagan symbolism including the sanctity of the number thirteen and its tie-in with the menstrual calendar and thirteen became a contemptible number in the Christian world. How many sat down to the Last Supper? Thirteen. And the first to leave was Judas who betrayed Christ. This led to the superstition that the first or perhaps the last to leave the table would die or suffer some misfortune within the year. Many still believe it is unlucky to sit down at a table of thirteen.

Because there were twelve apostles, in early Christian numerology anything that went beyond twelve was considered sinful. And some say that thirteen was deemed unlucky since human beings first began to count. They added their ten fingers and two feet and got twelve, and what came after twelve was a mystery and amounted to terror of the unknown.

What I want to know is why they didn't count their toes! If they did, that might have made the number twenty-three unlucky.

The fear of the number thirteen became so great that a word was created for it: Triskaidekaphobia, which literally translates to "three and ten fear." Ever ride in an elevator and notice the missing thirteenth floor? Ever hear the terms "baker's dozen" or "devil's dozen?" I read other accounts that credited the Romans with associating thirteen with death and misfortune. The Roman year consisted of twelve months and each of their days was a daytime or nighttime of twelve hours. The Romans considered twelve a number of completeness and thirteen dangerously exceeded proper limits.

After leaving the bookstores with an armful of heavy tomes, I also spoke with a woman named Myrddian, whom I met through a mutual friend. Myrddian said she wasn't a witch, but a "student of the occult."

Myrddian explained that the mystique of Friday the Thirteenth was steeped like an herbal teabag in the world of the occult. She said the occult breaks down everything into numbers. "Thirteen is three and one, which makes the powerful number four," she said. "First of all, it's a square and the four equal sides of a square represent the four elements of water, earth, fire and air along with the directions north, east, south and west."

Who knew?

She further explained that the number four in the Tarot stands for leadership, aggression and worldliness and is represented by the emperor. Myrddian called Friday the Thirteenth a "bonus day." Like the witches, she had a reason to see some good in both elements of the phenomenon.

With a scented candle flickering in the background of her dimly lit apartment, she unwrapped a well-worn set of Tarot cards from a purple silk scarf and handed them to me to acquire my vibes—or something. My inclination was to shuffle and deal out seven cards each for a game of Go Fish, but she took them back from me. And before giving me a reading, she sorted through the cards and pulled out the Tarot trump numbered thirteen. She held it up and I shuddered. Thirteen is the ominous death card, illustrated with and represented by a skeleton mowing a field of human heads with a scythe.

"Don't be afraid," she said in the voice of Morticia Addams. "This card is a symbol of death as well as new life. It represents a transformation. As with all the cards, it's up to you to interpret trump number thirteen as good or bad."

After my reading, which I interpreted as all good, thank you very much, Myrddian talked about Friday. She called it the day of Venus and said that rituals are performed on Fridays to keep rhythm with beauty and art. "Venus protects nature's balance, physical perfection and harmony. It represents fertility of plants, animals, humans and the end of a barren phase," she said.

Rituals are an important part of all religious ceremonies, from Christianity to the occult. Myrddian told me that a ritual performed on Friday the Thirteen might include an offering to Venus or to Earth. She suggested using green and pink candles and placing flowers on an altar as a tribute to the beauty of Venus. "Or you can take a bath with herbs like rose petals or jasmine, adding certain spices you might find in your own kitchen that represent Venus," she said.

I checked my spice cabinet to see if I had any Venus spices and I was delightfully surprised. Alas, I had no Balm of Gilead, mugwort, or quassia chips, but I did have thyme. And I learned that thyme's powers are: Health, healing, sleep, psychic powers, love, purification and courage. The parts to use are the leaves and flowers and it will magically attract good health if you burn it or wear it.

Concocting a recipe is a lot like performing a ritual. In fact, Myrddian compared the shaping of a ritual to making a cake. "To make a cake you don't just will it into action," she said. "You add a variety of ingredients to get the result you want. If you want coconut flavor, you add coconut. But in a ritual if you want good health and love, you add a little rosehips."

She offered advice for behavior on Friday the Thirteenth, suggesting a stabilization of things in my life and keeping the status quo in balance. "It's a good time to break old habits or dissolve a bad relationship," she said. Then she blew out the candle and opened the heavy curtains and my eyeballs shrunk to the size of pinheads. Through my squint, her pale skin appeared luminous and I found her to be quite beautiful. As she showed me to the door, she warned me to be careful in my research. "It's easy to get lost in the mystical world of the occult because there's so much reading material available," she said. "Don't forget there's a real world out there and a lot of bad luck is simply the result of mundane communication snags!"

I thanked her and then gave her a wry smile. I wasn't worried about having bad luck. I knew I had already uttered the words "rabbit, rabbit, rabbit" on the first day of the month.

Baby Showers on the Brain

March 1, 1991

Everyone around me is reproducing. It's like my own personal baby boom where due dates are written all over my calendar. Yet except for newspaper deadlines, none of these dates pertain to me. My only contribution to this baby boom is to help keep the local baby shower gift shops in business.

"And when is it going to be your turn?" I'm always asked, which is the real noise made by a ticking biological clock.

"Three years," I say with a careful blend of casualness and certainty. Heavier on the certainty. I've been responding "three years" for at least six. It just seems like a good way to let someone know that you're not against having babies but you're just not ready right now.

So, I'm doing what every modern, educated, childless, married woman does. I'm taking lessons on this reproduction thing by attending baby showers.

Since my unofficial registration at the U of M (that's University of Maternity, of course), small, hand-addressed pink and blue invitations keep cropping up in my mailbox like so much junk mail from computer software companies who keep getting my name from some list.

Baby showers have become my main form of getting together with the girls. Gone are the slumber parties, cheerleading practices and white wine happy hours. We're following the trends of our decades.

You know the old jump rope game, " ... first comes love, than comes

115

marriage ..." The games we play now make us guess things pertaining to weight gain and inches grown. Gift giving, however, is still the highlight of the party. The recent or experienced mothers always give the most practical gifts. They are the ones to learn from.

"Oh you'll need that for sure," they say when the care package of thermometers, baby Tylenol and booger-suckers are opened.

Novices like me, on the other hand, load up the mothers-to-be with darling outfits (which we might buy for ourselves if they were made in larger—much larger—sizes). Or we buy books, stuffed toys or picture frames. Nice stuff, but not very practical. We'll learn, the mothers assure us. They're great teachers.

Some of the newest mothers even bring example babies. These babies, dressed in their own shower gift outfits, enable us to coo at their cuteness and sigh at the smelly-yet-loving responsibility of diaper changing. Breastfeeding, too, is always a hit.

March is the heaviest month for expectations in my little baby boom. So far I've received two calls bearing the news of actual stork droppings: A girl named Emma Jane, who happens to be my newest niece, and a boy named Scott Christopher, born to very dear friends.

Each of them will be getting an adorable stuffed lamb from me. And who knows? This little lamb may end up the equivalent of Lionus' blanket to one of these kids!

Meanwhile, Gina, Sue, Cynthia, Lisa, Blanca, Julie and Marlena, I'm waiting on news from all of you.

After the Vasectomy

My answer to the question of when we intended to reproduce should have been four years instead of three. Four years after I wrote this piece, we finally felt ready to go for it. By this time we had left California and moved to the Northwoods of Wisconsin. When we first arrived, mere babes in the woods, we didn't want to complicate our decision to start a new business together with an actual baby. So, we did what a lot of childless married couples do. We got dogs.

My puppies were my babies. (How many times have you heard childless couples claim, "our dogs are our kids?") I prepared a special "nursery" for them in the basement, filled it with blankets and squeaky toys and wrapped a tick-tock clock in their bedding to simulate their own mother's heartbeat at night. I awoke from a light slumber, as one ear tuned into the bowels of the house, and walked down the stairs to hold and comfort them during the equivalent of a two o'clock feeding.

From a litter of hybrid wolves, these puppies were like adopting children with special needs. Dakotah, tri-colored with white, beige and black looked like her mother, the husky/timber wolf; and Luna, who was pure white with light green eyes, looked just like her father the shepherd / arctic wolf, were very challenging. We were warned about this before taking them on, even "interviewed" by the breeders. But we were certain we could handle them.

Determined to be a good mommy, I brushed their soft, lanolin-like coats each day and taught them how to walk with leashes. One was smart and feisty, always ready to romp on her sister and bite her ears. The other was moody and stubborn to stay wild and untrained. (Funny, I could describe my two children the exact same way.) The day I collared Luna, the stubborn one, with a choke chain, she would have rather suffocated than have her spirit broken. I yanked and pulled, clicked and cajoled and it was days of struggle before she stopped fighting the leash. It's just like my younger daughter who has no fear of consequences. She doesn't care if the entire neighborhood hears her hissy fit in the morning when her new jacket doesn't fit just right or she's wearing "the wrong" shoes.

I think raising the wolves was better training for taking care of babies than attending shower classes at the University of Maternity in earlier years; however, I abandoned my responsibility with the dogs when our children came, as my focus transferred from the kennel to the nursery. Luna and Dakotah took a permanent backseat to my own breed.

• • •

The Things I Wish I'd Said

My Irish-twin sister, Gayle, hosted a baby shower for me when I had only just begun to "show." At my request we didn't play any games like "guess the fat girl's weight" or "guess what strained vegetable is on your tongue while blindfolded." I had reached the category of "advanced age mother," so I felt a more sophisticated baby shower was in order.

There weren't any example babies; however, we had a few adolescent children in the room, and a lot of mothers making comments like, "they didn't have anything called a Diaper Genie when I was changing those damn things."

Since I was the last of my siblings to reproduce and close to the last of my friends who intended to have children to actually have them, I don't think I've attended a baby shower since my own. The baby shower invitations and pretty little birth announcements that followed no longer decorate the face of my refrigerator. Instead they've been replaced with invitations to birthday parties. Kid's birthday parties, my latest room in hell, seem to happen just about every weekend. And while I'm grateful my children are popular enough to receive invitations, I'm often relieved when we have a conflict.

I've done Chuck E. Cheese's version of a birthday party exactly once. Never again. Those big, H.R. Puff-n-Stuff-type creatures singing on stage gave my daughter a pretty good scare. Plus, there were too many drippy noses and with my mother-vision, I actually saw the germs multiplying on the cage of saliva balls and handles of the games guaranteed to spew out streams of tickets for the kids to trade in for a bunch of plastic crap that ends up in the cracks of my furniture.

Then there are the roller skating birthday parties, which are basically Chuck E. Cheese's on wheels, where you must protect your children from adolescent skaters zooming around the turns like the Green Hornet. On that note, I don't remember "learning" how to skate. I swear I must have been born knowing how to stay upright on skates and I think it came from growing up in the Midwest. In that part of the country we, like Hans Brinker, strapped on our silver skates as soon as the creeks froze over or the local parks flooded their baseball fields. Replacing the blades with wheels when the ice melted was just a natural progression. But my daughters, who haven't experienced a real winter season since they could walk let alone skate, definitely had to be taught.

The thing I detest most about kids' birthday parties, besides having to shop for and spend money on the presents (my spending criteria dropped from twenty to fifteen bucks), is that each ends with what's known as a "party bag." Perhaps a better name for these bags is a "candy bag," because inevitably that's what fills them. Lots and lots of candy. And I eat my heart out every time one of these parties features a piñata.

The last piñata we had at one of our kid's parties was not a donkey or a star with streamers. It was a near perfect replica of my four-year-old. She spotted it one day at the Safeway and stared at the yellow hair, blue eyes and pink dress and just like Narcissus staring in the pond, fell madly in love. "I want that for my birrrrrrttthday," she whined. "Plllleeeeease?" The resemblance was uncanny and it was too funny not to buy, so we did. Then at the party, as the effigy of our little girl hung from the rafters of our patio, we watched as twenty-five kids took turns trying to decapitate it. It was downright perverse!

Keeping candy away from my kids is a full-time job done completely in vain. I'm not sure when it happened, but every calendar holiday has somehow become an opportunity to get candy. A plastic pumpkin filled with candy at Halloween is understandable and even an Easter Basket with chocolate bunnies and marshmallow peeps is okay. But when, for example, did Valentine's Day become more about passing out pure sugar hearts than paper valentine cards? Christmas ornaments are now boring if not in the shape of a candy cane that my kids can eat while they're dreaming of sugarplums. And even the Lac du Flambeau, Wisconsin Fourth of July parade has the kids scrambling to the street to get their hands on candy thrown from people riding on the floats.

My husband and I coach an under-six soccer team and for many of them, the game isn't about kicking the ball into the goal. It's about what they're going to get as a snack after the game. And my kids tend to ask, "what's for dessert," before they even sit down to the evening meal. It's either that or "*how much more bites* do I have to eat before I get candy?"

The Things I Wish I'd Said

...

At the baby showers we attended before our children were born, when we discussed the monumentally important environmental issue of cloth versus disposable diapers and the benefits of breast milk over formula, we didn't think ahead to the more perplexing issues that would forever plague our futures—the issues that would creep up as we started to lose control of our helpless, darling infants. In our desire to create a new generation of human beings we had a lot of support from those who had been through it before us and knew the importance of arming us with tools like Diaper Genies, receiving blankets, A and D Ointment and thermometers. But now that the kids are growing up, we've stopped throwing parties for each other and started throwing candy at them during their own parties.

We get advice where we can from other moms at the bus stop or from older sisters during lengthy phone conversations, and some of us who have the time can invest in a whole series of books tailored to raising our toddlers, adolescents and teenagers. Some of us even need advice now on how to get our college graduates out of the house as they try to save money for the future by continuing to spend ours.

Although I didn't move back in with my parents after graduating from college, maybe I too was slow to mature, which is perhaps why I waited so long to give birth. I don't believe I truly became an adult until the day I had a baby and experienced that thing called "mother-love."

I remember talking with my friend Gina shortly after her daughter was born and she tried to explain the feeling of motherhood and the concept of mother-love. "How can I put it," she mused. "It's like this: If my daughter were somehow stranded on a train track and I was forced to jump in front of a speeding train to save her life, I'd do it without hesitation. I can't say I'd do the same thing if it were my husband laying on that track."

It can be that dramatic. When my first child was born it felt like a christening. I found myself thinking about God and creation and miracles with every coo, every gurgle and even every diaper change. From the first moment my six-pound, twelve-ounce daughter looked into my face, with a look so wise and so sure that she was exactly where she was meant to be, which was out of that womb and on top of my pillow-soft stomach, I realized I'd never be the same.

Mother-love is a physical ache. In a mother's eyes, there's nothing more beautiful than her children. It's a thirst we quench with a hug and hunger we feed with a kiss. It's a pride so rich seeing her perform a piano piece and sing confidently into the microphone that we only hear the notes she actually hits. And when she releases her clutch from our pant legs and ventures out to the soccer field and actually stays there long enough to get her foot on the ball as it rolls past her, we feel as though she just scored the winning goal at the World Cup. And when she tells us she doesn't really want to run around the whole track in the "Chariots of Fire," event at her school's Field Day but does it anyway, and finishes the race without stopping ahead of most of her classmates—even after her shoes have fallen off—we feel as out of breath with joy as if *we* had just successfully run that long race on a hot day in the desert. Even when she's home from school sick with a fever on a day where all our morning plans are shot to hell, and she finally ambles out of her bedroom at noon with linen creases on her face, wrinkled pajamas and disheveled hair, all we see is the fact that she's walking on her toes, and that her previously pouting lips have formed into a smile at the first sight of us, our hearts feel like they could pop right out of our chests.

Such is my take on this hard-to-explain feeling. And since I'd stake my life on the fact that my husband feels the same, I should perhaps call it, parent-love rather than mother-love.

I'm not sorry we waited to have our babies. Giving up any concept of a life or plans for a life I might have had in order to focus on the lives I helped to create has been a bigger reward than I could have imaged back when I attended all those baby showers. Now that I've reached a certain age, friends have stopped asking if we plan to have another baby, or more precisely, "don't you want to go for the boy?" And again, I'm not sorry we limited our brood to two. We are blessed with two healthy, gorgeous girls and two is enough. "One for each of us," we like to say at times when we're required to get them to the afternoon's activities on opposite ends of town— or separate the fight over who really won the game of Chutes and Ladders.

The Things I Wish I'd Said

In simple terms, for me motherhood means that my life will never again be only about me. There's never a moment when my babies are not on my brain.

Chapter 3
Not Too Political

Some praise at morning what they blame at night,

but always think the last opinion right.

—**Alexander Pope,** *An Essay on Criticism*

The Wasp and Mr. Alger

November 5, 1991

Two years ago I attended a conference at UC-Berkeley for writers called "Women Writers at Work." It was an all-day event held in a lecture hall packed with the gender opposite of the United States Senate, about a hundred women and a couple of men.

On the speaking agenda that day were such distinguished names as Sue Miller, Amy Tan, Harriett Doerr and Isabel Allende. Each spoke of her experience as a writer, and most read passages from published works.

They were a very entertaining group.

Aside from that little yen inside all of us that makes us want to meet our idols, my purpose in attending this event was for the encouragement I knew these talented women would deliver. They talked about the loneliness of writing, known by writers of both sexes, but they also focused on specific issues women writers face—especially women who have homes and children to take care of and who are constantly justifying their work.

Each mentioned that her success was based on a lot of persistence, a bit of luck, timing and connections.

"Hang in there. Keep plugging," was the message of the day.

The seminar was going very well. The audience was bright, responsive. We laughed at all the right places and avoided the typical cliché questions often posed to authors: "What writers influenced you?" and "Is your writing autobiographical?"

125

The Things I Wish I'd Said

As the hours passed, I felt I became part of an exceptional community. I had support. My work was justified. I believed I was going to go home that evening and compose my best work ever.

But those feelings were crushed in the middle of the last speaker's presentation.

Isabel Allende, best-selling author of *The House of Spirits, Eva Luna* and other novels, is Chilean and the niece of assassinated President Salvador Allende. She was slotted as the last speaker of the day—the grand finale.

At the time of the seminar, she lived in the Bay Area with her new husband, whom she married because she said she "loved his smell."

She is a wonderful speaker. A pretty woman, with short dark hair and dancing brown eyes, she moved about the speaking platform like a television talk show host, a colorful scarf flowing in her wake, big silver jewelry sparkling in the florescent light. She was as enchanting as the characters she had written about: Clara the Clairvoyant, Rosa the Beautiful.

Allende brought to life the magical stories of her childhood including furniture that moved around her house by the power of telekinesis. Nobody needed to ask whether or not her stories were autobiographical. "It really happened!" she insisted.

Nobody needed to ask, either, which authors she read. She offered this information freely, perhaps as part of her presentation.

"I read women," she said. "But they're Black, Hispanic or Chinese." And then she paused briefly. I want to believe she closed her eyes so she didn't see the faces of the mostly Caucasian admirers looking at her as she added the following forceful words:

"Waspy literature is DEAD!"

At this statement, I gasped so loudly that I didn't hear or notice if anyone else was as taken aback as me. But personally, I was jilted. The only thing not reeking WASP from me is that I was baptized Catholic—and since the 1975 publishing of John R. Powers' novels *Do Black Patent Leather Shoes Really Reflect Up?* and *The Last Catholic in America*, what new material can be written about the predicament of growing up Catholic?

I gathered by Allende's statement that unless you have suffered the plight of poverty, racial discrimination or political coups, or had relatives who could make furniture float, you had nothing to write about anymore.

Do we WASPs or WASP-types really have nothing more to say? Is each of us that ordinary or boring? Have all our stories been told? Allende seemed to contend that anything ending with "And they lived happily ever after" was worthless. Unless, of course, the characters had to scratch and scrape to achieve this happiness.

Horatio Alger stories are always good for the soul; however, life—no matter who you are or what color your skin is—provides many, many stories. And to proclaim that one form of literature, a form based on race and creed, is "dead" was highly irresponsible.

I left the seminar with my head down. Like a typical WASP, I suppose, I wanted my money back.

My Fascinating Life

Three things. Number one: As of this writing, the United States Senate has gained twelve more women, bringing the total from two to fourteen. Number two: I have become a full-fledged WASP by leaving the Catholic Church for the catholic-lite, or protestant faith of the Episcopal Church. And three: I haven't read anything by Isabel Allende since that seminar. I actually bought the book, *Paula,* which is a memoir written at the bedside of her comatose daughter, but found I couldn't get past the first few pages of more flying furniture and what I thought would be a heart-wrenching ever after.

I'm ashamed to admit I'm holding a grudge against her. I attended that conference to commiserate, er, I mean, bond with fellow female writers. But I guess I held myself in too high a place, arrogantly believing that by the end of the day, the above-mentioned writers would somehow become my peers.

They weren't my peers.

I wanted them to be my mentors and learn from them all the secrets of success. But Allende, for one, assured me in no uncertain terms that I had no place in her world.

Alas, as if I needed anyone to tell me again, as a writer I work alone. Every workshop or conference I've attended, or every nonfiction account of a writer's life I've read reminds me that writing is Solitaire without the deck of cards and a road trip without a map to a place you've never been. Like brushing your teeth, watching your weight or dare I say, masturbating, we writers are like Lee Harvey Oswald. We act alone.

Okay. At least I *try* to work alone. The trick of finding uninterrupted time to bond with my computer is currently my biggest challenge. I'm supposed to work in the guesthouse, known in some circles as a "pouting house," but in our corner of the country it's a *casita*, which is Spanish for "little house." It's a detached unit located some one hundred feet from our back door. When Midwestern guests escaping the raunchy winters do not occupy it, it stands vacant and is equipped with a lovely Mexican-made desk and a G3 computer with tons of storage space on the hard drive. While furnishing this little house, I called it "my office," and imagined setting up hours—real hours where during those hours, I'd respect my work as if I had punched a time clock. But if I stay out there too long and get caught up in something, I might forget that I have children and that I need to get them out of bed, dressed and fed in less than an hour. Let's not forget that I, too, need to get out of my robe and myself out the door for a day's worth of volunteer activities, including driving my child to choir practice at the church an hour before the service, and an afternoon fashion show where, God help me, I'm going to model cruise wear that the store clerks say is so fabulous, that "they should make a cruise for that dress."

So much for writing today.

There's always a reason for not making writing my top priority. So, from where I sit—dead-ass-center in the house (where a mommy belongs)—plucking away on my overstuffed iBook (read laptop computer), I hear my youngest child contemplating a study in C on the piano. Occasionally she leans toward a version of "Mary Had A Little Lamb," and I can't help but get caught up in the tune. Thinking of my next sentence, bright colors swirl in the peripheral vision of my right eye and suddenly, I'm on my feet and headed toward the refrigerator—not to fetch a cold glass of lemonade, although I could use one, but to rearrange those annoying refrigerator magnets for the third time this month. Organizing the kids' artwork competes with the less colorful paperwork catching the corner of my left eye that comes into this house daily in the form of bills, insurance policies and financial statements. They actually throb with the pulse of a life that spans either ten or thirty days before it's too late and they're past due. And on that note, I also hear snippets of a telephone conversation my husband is having with one of his pocket-full of financial advisors or planners, and I drift off wondering whether or not we still have enough money to make next month's mortgage let alone pay all those pesky bills.

Man, this stuff is rich! What was Isabel Allende talking about? This is the fascinating life of a WASPy writer and what I've chosen to write about. And who knows? I may get lucky and find an audience—or even luckier and the furniture will start floating around in my living room. Then I'll have something to write about that even Isabel Allende might find interesting.

Backlash Whiplash

April 14, 1992

backlash ('bak-lash) n. 1: A sudden violent backward movement or reaction. 3: a strong adverse reaction (as to a recent political or social development).

whiplash ('hwip-lash) n.1. the lash of a whip. 2: something resembling a blow from a whip.

There's been a lot of talk lately about a backlash against women and the women's movement in this country. Much of it has been in the media, citing Pulitzer prize-winning, former Wall Street Journal reporter Susan Faludi, and her book *Backlash: The Undeclared War Against American Women*.

This 552-page bestseller lists example after example, statistic after statistic to support the claim that the women's movement is being sabotaged by a highly effective campaign to discredit its achievements and distort its message.

Faludi points her witty, sharp pen at the government, the silver screen and the mass media for hurling the accusation that feminism is "responsible for every woe besetting women, from mental depression to meager savings accounts, from teenage suicides to eating disorders to bad complexions."

When I read this book a few months back, I turned the pages as though it were a potboiler romance or psychological thriller. The words before me felt familiar—almost like my own.

The Things I Wish I'd Said

Shortly after the Thomas-Hill sexual harassment case when the fire of feminism flared inside me like never before, I overheard a young (twentysomething) bright woman say in conversation, "I'm not a feminist or anything but . . . " I didn't know what she was talking about nor did I hear what came after the "but," because (rude as it was) I lunged at her, making her answer to the "I'm not a feminist" part.

Without the slightest hesitation, she equated feminism with radicalism—with marching in the street. She failed to mention (and therefore understand?) the ideology itself.

At some point during the 1980s, the ideology of feminism lost its meaning. The term "feminist" went from signifying simply a supporter of political, economic and social equality of the sexes, to a dated image of "bra burners" or women (who supposedly wanted to be men) who had made false promises to a generation of young women about equality, causing them only the added burden of "doing it all."

While the successes of the women's movement helped to make it possible for women to attain the higher education needed for successful, well-paying careers in the 1980s, most of what we were hearing and reading about were things like "women's burnout." The movies we saw included crazed career women freaking out over their noisy biological clocks.

Just before I read Faludi's book, I was in a movie theater awaiting the start of Oliver Stone's *JFK* when a promo for the surprise hit, *The Hand That Rocks the Cradle* came on the screen. Usually, I'm not one to hiss at promos—a sound I've gotten quite used to in movie theaters since living in the oh-so-politically-correct Bay Area—but I couldn't help myself. Here, I thought, was yet another deranged woman in a childcare crisis movie.

Then I sat through *JFK* and watched the white male political machine in action with the phallic symbol to top all phallic symbols—the Washington Monument—in the background. In that theater, I contemplated a lot more than whether or not Lee Harvey Oswald acted alone.

I've spent my entire life believing that all people were created equal. I've had strong role models—both female and male—who nurtured these beliefs and enabled me to grow strong and self-confident. I've always been grateful to Gloria Steinem and the feminists of the 1970s who helped me to become the kind of woman that many capable, frustrated women before my time only dreamed of becoming.

And now every time progress takes a step backward due to the backlash defined by Faludi, my head snaps back in surprise. Indeed, this assault on women's rights feels like whiplash.

I'm fed up. And if being a feminist truly does denote the need to march in the streets, I'm putting on my boots.

The SAHD Truth

The man in my house does the cooking, the grocery shopping and most of the laundry. He makes the kids' lunches and walks them to the school bus. He volunteers in their classrooms, coaches soccer and gets them to and from birthday parties, piano lessons and dance class.

He is my husband. And he is my equal.

Big surprise: In the last ten years I've learned that the women's movement—and even the backlash against it—hasn't been as much about women's attitudes as it has been about the attitudes of men. Since the days of the suffragists, and most likely prior to that, women have been so far ahead of men in terms of equality awareness, that we've had to give men time to catch up. I'm going to go out on a limb and say that I think men have finally caught up. And by this I mean *most* men. Anyone with the name Richard, for example, who is this side of no longer using the nickname "Dick," has essentially graduated from the class of equal rights between men and women. Of course, there are Neanderthal cases roaming the streets who venture into our proportional spheres and have no clue they're dealing with an equal. And I'm not only referring to men who go by the name Grandpa and treat anyone younger than them as a mere amusement. I'm referring to the occasional soccerdad, who is incapable of addressing you by your first name or letting you complete a sentence during a heated discussion about scheduling soccer practices for kindergartners.

"If you'll just listen to me a second and let me explain why I've scheduled our practices at . . ."

"No, you listen to ME!" he shouts. "I am a very busy man and my afternoons are filled with meetings. This is an incredible inconvenience."

"Yes, but I . . ."

"I KNOW you've been coaching for years and this is how *you* like to do it, but let's poll the parents to see if they are in agreement with me that practices should be held at five o'clock instead of four o'clock. (Unlike you and your husband) most people *do* work and this is, after all, about the kids."

"Huh?" I say, pulling the receiver away from my face and looking at the dots on the speaker area like they might spell out in Morse code what that stupid statement meant.

I almost hung up. Meanwhile, during this phone conversation my husband sat in the room pretending to read the newspaper. But one eye was glued to me as I paced the hardwood floors with a firm grip on the portable phone. I kept looking at him with big, can-you-believe-this eyes and mouthing the words, "*you* talk to this jerk!" I couldn't help but believe the Neanderthal might be more reasonable with another man. As he continued to rant, I pushed the hold button. "This guy says he's calling on behalf of the kids," I said.

"He's calling on behalf of himself!" said my equal.

"Will you talk to him?"

"No way," said Equal. "You're doing a great job. Just hold your ground and finish it."

When I pushed the hold button again, he still raged and failed to notice he'd been on hold for at least thirty seconds. Finally, he took a breath. "Finished?" I asked.

And then I finished the conversation. I told him I understood he was a very busy and important person but that my time was just as valuable, even though as a volunteer I worked for free. I further stated that my husband and I, without question, performed the community service of coaching soccer *for the kids.* "Here in Tucson, our life is all about raising our kids. You and your child can choose to be a part of that or we'll find you another team."

My husband and I are equals in the home and we are business partners. We own a family-style resort, a business that is finally profitable. It took eight years of blood, sweat and cold, hard cash investments before we made it into the black, but we're currently looking at a sustaining operation. The resort is located some two thousand miles away from Tucson in the state of Wisconsin, a place that might as well be Siberia in the minds of many desert dwellers. And because our Tucson neighbors don't see the resort or us working at it, it's easier for them to believe we simply don't work. And this has raised eyebrows since the work of taking care of two young children and volunteering time at their schools, in the church and on the soccer field doesn't merit much respect from the outside world.

In Wisconsin, however, we're justified, hardworking American citizens. During the summer we run the resort (meaning we make beds, scrub toilets and fix things), but business slows down dramatically in the winter—from one hundred percent occupancy to, if we're lucky, twenty percent. So, the low demand enables us to get away to our desert oasis where we focus on raising our children.

I can't help but think there's something wrong with a society that looks more favorably upon people who scrub toilets versus people who look after children.

There are certain scrutinizing questions we're all asked regarding our work. Professions allow people to paint a clear picture of you—whether or not you wear a uniform—so they know how to talk about you in private. Like, "since he's a computer programmer, maybe I can call him to help me with the nagging problem I'm having with my printer." Or " since he's a neurosurgeon, perhaps I should talk to him about my sister's neighbor's cousin's best friend's brain tumor." Say you're a housewife (does the term househusband even exist?) and that's a guaranteed way to get people to believe your lack of gainful employment makes you dull enough to not even talk about in private. The social calls you'll receive most often are from volunteer organizations looking for help since you clearly have nothing better to do.

When I was a university student, nearly every introduction included the question, "What's your major?" We joked about it as the quintessential college pick-up line or at the very least, a safe bet when there was nothing more to talk about besides the weather; but truthfully, we wanted to know. We wanted to categorize and plan accordingly. We knew engineering students spent a lot of time with their noses in math and physics books and weren't a sure bet to join you as a last minute date for that extra concert ticket burning a fifteen dollar hole in your flimsy pocket; film and/or photography majors drove funky cars or motorcycles and would inevitably ask you to model for them in some artsy-fartsy format; and history or political science majors would always get in on a juicy debate, that is when they weren't heavily into a game of Risk.

But today in our world outside the textbooks that taught us to define ourselves, the question has become "What do you *do*?" (We don't even say "for a living" any more, as it's tacit to this question.) And in spite of the strides we've made toward gender equality, more often and much to my chagrin, I still hear: "What does your *husband* do for a living?"

Sometimes I like to tell people I do nothing. Other times I spread my arms wide in a "here-I-am" manner and respond to the what-do-you-do question by saying, "You're looking at it." And in a "so's yer old man" manner, I add that my husband doesn't do anything either. I've come up with a variety of answers to please myself and make the questioner say one of two things. One: "Good for you!" (I love people who say this), or two: "Must be nice!" (Some people hate it when you're happy). In one breath my husband says he doesn't care what people think; yet in another breath he believes some people look down on him for his winter occupation as "Mr. Mom."

He's not alone in his choice of staying home to raise the kids. His numbers are growing. The most recent statistic I've seen is that there are some two million men who list their occupations as "stay at home dads." They even have an organization called SAHD and a host of websites dedicated to the issues that kick stay-at-home dads right in the balls. They're the same issues stay-at-home moms have faced for years, like isolation, the frustration of unrealized dreams and a genuine lack of respect from a society that thinks they can't make it in the working world. Betty Friedan documented all this in 1963 in her book *The Feminine Mystique*. But now that men are experiencing these emotions, well it's not a mystique. It's just SAHD. It reminds me of the joke I read in a forwarded email the other day, that if men gave birth, morning sickness would rank as the nation's number one health problem *and* there'd be a cure for stretch marks.

Some complained that radical feminists wouldn't be satisfied until we turned our men into women. Well, we've succeeded on that front and now all we have is a bigger group doing all the bitching. Raising kids is hard work and no one really knows this until they do it. Stay-at home-dads are just discovering this concept. Nevertheless, I applaud the development of these testosterone-based organizations. If having dads stay home helps raise well-adjusted, confident kids, and studies show that it does, as far as I'm concerned they can start shaving clubs or sell tools to each other at Tupperware-like parties.

Meanwhile, I want the moms out there to acknowledge my husband's contributions to the family and the school. He wasn't even invited to the volunteer lunch at the elementary school last spring and he had certainly donated time to the classroom. (I asked him and he came along anyway).

I believe for some women, men will always be aliens. We may have demanded a place in "their" world, but we still haven't made a place for them in ours'. Just once I'd like to hear that someone at the grocery store has asked my husband while he's sorting through his shopping list and telling the kids to put back the candy or cereal boxes, "And what does your *wife* do for a living?"

Hopefully, he'll put on a SAHD expression and say, "the same thing as I."

Can We Talk?

October 15, 1991

I'm almost relieved that the charge of sexual harassment came up against Supreme Court nominee, Clarence Thomas.

It's not because I was particularly for or against his confirmation. It's because through this circus they call the Senate Judiciary Committee hearing, I don't think we got the chance to learn much about him except that he grew up poor. We don't really know how he feels about abortion or civil rights because he would not answer questions directly.

We can only assume that with his Catholic upbringing he will be the nail in the coffin of Roe vs. Wade, which has me shaking in my boots. And because he is black, we desperately want to believe that civil rights will not suffer during his tenure. Oh, how we want to believe.

But now the question of discrimination based on sexual harassment of one Anita Hill has finally turned the real interrogation spotlight up bright on the character of Clarence Thomas.

The very fact that this potentially damaging charge has come out only now, at the eleventh hour as they say, is alarming. Members of the committee who were in favor of sweeping this issue under the rug, who were angered by the "leak" of the FBI investigation, have called Hill's allegations "a smear."

Hill is a tenured law professor, a graduate of Yale Law School—Thomas' alma mater—who has the support of her colleagues and students at the University of Oklahoma. She has nothing to gain and much to lose by coming forward with her side of the story. The idea that she would be discredited and not taken seriously is outrageous.

President Bush himself went as far as to say he was "unconcerned" by the allegations. Why? What does he know that we don't? Was he in the room when Thomas allegedly made sexually explicit remarks to her and retold scenes from porno flicks? I don't think so.

So, as with most cases of sexual harassment, it's his word against hers. Thomas, of course, has flatly denied the charges.

Sexual harassment in the workplace has been defined as "unwelcome behavior of a sexual nature." It may involve a threat or it could mean acts or statements creating a hostile work environment. Unfortunately it's up to you to define the boundaries of what offends you. And often men and women have different standards. One man's form of flattery may be one women's idea of hostility.

According to the N.O.W. Legal Defense League, twenty percent of working women report having experienced sexual harassment in the workplace and only six percent have actually filed complaints. No one really wants to have her character and integrity scrutinized or her career potentially ruined. It's as unpleasant and embarrassing as the harassment itself.

I know this for a fact.

I had a boss once who left town in the middle of a huge project. All the decisions and pressing deadlines were left to me. I accepted the responsibility.

The boss returned (at the eleventh hour) and immediately started making changes—subjective decisions I thought were totally unnecessary. When I objected, a discussion—okay, it was a fight—ensued. The boss stormed out of the room and brooded away the afternoon behind a closed door while I continued working. Before I left, however, I decided to clear things up by knocking on the boss' door.

After the initial awkwardness, I was thanked for making the first move and then complimented on my work. The issue, I was told, was that I was very good at my job, perhaps too good, and this was a threat. (Did I have higher aspirations? Did I want to take over the company?) I quelled these concerns and said "thanks" for the compliments.

The boss said, "You're welcome," and then made a comment that I'm still too embarrassed to print. But it was about my body and it stunned me because one minute I was a competent, professional worker and the next I was reduced to nothing more than ... It was humiliating.

What was even worse about this scene was that my boss was a woman. Boy was I confused. Was I supposed to slap a lawsuit on her or simply slap her face? I did neither, but I have never forgotten this incident and the stress it caused.

I firmly believe that Anita Hill and whoever leaked the FBI report were right in bringing forth these charges to enable us to further examine the character of Clarence Thomas and the issue of sexual harassment.

It's time for this issue to be taken seriously.

Rape of the Issue

This issue has been taken seriously, all right. It's been taken to the cleaners, who've washed it, diluted it, worn it out and frankly, taken the fun right out of it.

Since the case of Clarence Thomas and Anita Hill, when sexual harassment stepped on the world stage and the bright lights of the mainstream media, there have been significant changes in the interpretation of sexual harassment laws by the Supreme Court; yet the Court still allows a lot of latitude in not only the definition of sexual harassment in educational and employment settings, but in proving cases. Most decisions are made on a case-by-case basis. So, even though there are laws in place, we are still not at the point where they are understood and embraced. We need to embrace laws before the threat of punishment for breaking them will change our behavior.

These days we can't even wink at each other without being accused of sexual harassment. Most adults are capable of telling the difference between an innocent flirtation and a legitimate case of harassment; but now we have the opportunity to abuse the laws and use the claim of sexual harassment as a weapon of self-defense (or a vengeance). We've got young schoolgirls, for example, who once might have been flattered by a boy's attention, instead claiming sexual harassment when they want to get the boy in trouble.

As a schoolgirl, when I wanted to get my older brother in hot water I'd yell, "Mo-om, Tommy HIT me!" He might have shoved me out of the way, breathed (or farted) in my general direction, or taken the blue, Schwinn ten-speed I claimed as my own once he abandoned it, but all I had to do was yell "he HIT me!" and the trial was over. He lost and a vengeance was mine. This is typical adolescent behavior. Older brother smacks pesky younger sister, younger sister yells "HIT," older brother is in trouble. Simple, right?

It's not so simple when the new charge is sexual harassment.

I know a seventh grade boy who was accused of sexual harassment when he bent down to pick up a dropped pen and someone from afar shouted that he was looking up a girl's skirt. (He wasn't.) The embarrassed girl went to the authorities and the boy was formally charged. During his interrogation, where he was confined to a classroom alone with a police-man, he heard the most dreaded words a young student can hear: "This will be on your PERMANENT RECORD!" It's one thing to have the threat of a blotchy school record following you around the rest of your life, but the same threat from the lips of a cop brings with it a visual of mug shots and "priors." All that for dropping a pen!

The hormones inside the body of an average seventh grader are like a sack full of agitated bees on a warm, sweet-smelling day. At that age they've only just entered the world of sexual politics. It takes years of experience to find your place in that sticky world.

When I was in seventh grade sexual harassment was rampant, but we had no idea it had a name. The developed girls had to fend off a between-class hallway activity made up by the boys called "knobbing." The trick was to score points by somehow flattening a girl's boob—whether up against a locker, against someone else's body or by a more daring boy's hand. I was never a victim of knobbing, because I didn't start to develop until the time

I took my college entry exams. But that doesn't mean I wasn't a victim of sexual harassment. The knobbing boys were aware that I had no boobs to knob, so instead they hurled verbal insults calling me names. These names were so hurtful that I'd go home and fill my triple-A cup bra with cotton balls and imagine what life might be like as a girl who got knobbed. (I can't believe I actually fantasized about physical, sexual abuse!) We placed the opinions of boys in very high regard, and never dreamed of going to the authorities to discuss our feelings of belittlement.

And this is where Anita Hill has proved to be triumphant. While she was ultimately unsuccessful in her attempt to keep Clarence Thomas from getting to the Supreme Court, as he was approved as an associate justice by a Senate vote of 52-48, her courage in coming forth on this issue has made it possible for the rest of us to talk about it, define it, understand it and hopefully, embrace the laws meant to curtail it.

In 1996 Hill published a book called *Speaking Truth to Power* and has left the University of Oklahoma and now teaches social policy, law and women's studies at Brandeis University. She admits that the issue of sexual harassment has been her calling. She writes, "I did not choose the issue of sexual harassment; it chose me. And, having been chosen, I have come to believe that it is up to me to try and give meaning to it all."

But is it really up to Anita Hill to define the ambiguities of this broad issue? And is it possible for anyone to go beyond the Supreme Court's case-by-case system in the sexually charged world of he-said, she-said?

In 1991 I asked, "Can we talk?" Yep, thanks especially to Anita Hill, we can talk. We can talk this issue until we harass it to death.

Take Me Back To Tulsa

September 17, 1991

Don't you just want to shake people who are only twenty-one years old and are planning to get married? I don't mean planning some day like most young girls with white lace dreams; but those who are already planning such telltale things as china patterns and living room colors. With a big circle on next year's calendar during the month of June, they see nothing beyond that date—the BIG DAY.

Whenever I meet a very young person who is in the thick of prenuptial bliss, I'm at a loss for words. To say things to them like "congratulations," or "how wonderful!" would make me a hypocrite. And the things I want to say to them ("aren't you a little young?" or "please don't do it!") would make me . . . well, insensitive to say the least.

When I was twenty-two, I was one of those young girls who thought she was old enough and in love enough to get married. And I did.

I met my first husband during our freshman year of college. I thought he was the smartest person I had ever known. An engineering student, he taught me a great deal about things like physics and thermodynamics. And he was funny. He loved jazz and reggae music. He was quite artistic, always scribbling and making up political cartoons.

He was crazy about bicycles and rode his handmade bike everywhere. He even convinced me to ride from our college town in southern Illinois one summer north through the cornfields and Amish communities of central Illinois toward Chicago. Until my knee gave out somewhere north of Champaign, it was a wonderful adventure.

I would have followed him anywhere.

I remember we announced our engagement at my graduation party. The news received a mixed response. His family seemed happy about it, certainly not surprised. Yet the things that stand out in my mind now are things that I wish, then, I would have paid closer attention to.

One of my older sisters (the one who didn't get married at the age of twenty) started crying. She was single, in transition, and I thought she was disappointed that I was making an "old maid" out of her. My mother, who is usually quiet anyway, said nothing. The next day she told me that she was upset because she thought I should have told her the news first. That's the way it should have been, she said. Daughters are supposed to tell their mothers first.

I didn't know this.

Later that summer, before my beau and I packed up my '63 Dodge Dart and headed west to California with an envelope full a resumes, a stereo strapped to the roof and a thousand dollars between us, my mother made a comment about our relationship to which I wish I had listened.

I was arguing with my fiancé on the telephone, about what I can't really remember. I know I wasn't getting my way and that made me very mad. Having overheard bits of the conversation, my mother said, "Maybe, Michele, he isn't the right one for you."

I didn't pursue the issue. I drove away, far away. And in spite of several things that happened to us once we moved to California that would have indicated to any clear-thinking, mature person that a marriage between the two of us would be a mistake, we became Mr. and Mrs. soon-to-be-another-California-divorce-statistic after only a few short years. Actually, I remember being happy for about three weeks—the three weeks before his college roommate moved in with us.

It's a sad story, I know. But naturally, now that I'm very happily married to Mr. Right, I think the whole experience made me a stronger, wiser human being. Time has allowed me to heal the wounds of my first marriage. Thank goodness there's no bitterness between us and I'm even more grateful that there were no children involved. Unfortunately, I believe I'm one of the few lucky survivors of a too-young marriage.

For those who did find their "soul mates" at a young age and have enduring relationships and happy marriages, that's wonderful. "Congratulations" is the right word to say. Yet I still can't help myself from gagging whenever I meet that twenty-one year-old bride-to-be. Even if I boldly tried to discourage her, I'm sure my words would fall upon deaf ears.

So I just smile and say, "I hope you'll be very happy together."

I do.

The Disastrous First Marriage

My views on the subject of potential failure of youthful unions haven't changed. But today there's a term for it. It's called the Disastrous First Marriage, or DFM for short.

I had barely finished typing the period at the end of the above sentence when I noticed some action in my backyard. Lurking behind the walls where we house the pool equipment was the "pool lady." Some folks may have a "pool boy," a stud named Carlos who reaches a long pole into the depths of the Caribbean Blue pebble-tech swimming hole while his rippling six-pack abs shine brighter than the day-glo colors of his Speed-o. But I think that's only in the movies or in places where divorcées (or soon-to-be divorcées) actually have time to lounge around their pools, sip margaritas and suck on cigarettes through sleek, black cigarette holders while they eye up the hired help. Meanwhile, here in the real world—the arid subdivisions of the Sonoran Desert—we've got a young gal with a bright, Pepsodent smile and face full of freckles who faithfully shows up each week to clean and maintain our pool.

As she waded through the mound of noodles, giant ducks and rubber rafts to clear the channel for the drainage spout, I retrieved the latest invoice for basket, brush and once a month vacuuming service and brought it outside to show her. At once she tipped her blue ball cap and greeted me with an exuberant, "hi."

"I haven't paid this bill yet," I said, waving it in the air, "because I thought you said the paperwork would reflect the splitting of jobs between your new company name and the old."

"Yes, I did tell you that," she said, momentarily removing her cap and fingering her sun-bleached bangs. "But now my soon-to-be-ex is giving me a hard time. He's trying to keep the whole company."

"I see," I said, aware of her pending divorce. "Getting ugly is it?"

"You got that right," she said with a wry smile.

"It's called the DFM," I said.

"The DFM?"

"The Disastrous First Marriage. A lot of us were victims. Or better yet, survivors."

"No kidding," said the pool lady, still smiling. "Who knew?"

There are a lot of us who know about the disastrous first marriage. We're out there prowling around backyards and coffee shops, going to work, raising kids, volunteering in schools, cleaning pools and writing about the things we wish we'd said instead of "I do."

Oh, how I wish I'd said out loud the thoughts inside my head as my parents drove me to the remote country church where my first wedding took place. My first panicky thought as I sat stiffly in my Victorian lace was: "Stop the car and let me out." Failing to turn that thought into statement, my thoughts became more reasonable—something along the lines of, "Mom and Dad, do you think anyone would mind if I just didn't show up today?" I failed to utter that one, too.

I don't often talk about my DFM because frankly, it was so short and so long ago that I barely remember it. Well, that's not really true. You know how sometimes you'll come up with a story based on a childhood memory and then an older sibling or a parent will say, "You were far too young to remember that trip up the Fox River!" Maybe my first marriage was like that fabled trip up the Fox River and I was simply too young to really remember it. Well, it was definitely like a trip up *some* river. And it was the kind of trip where you're paddling upstream without the proverbial paddle.

My DFM is a memory I conveniently repress. So, when the fact that it *is* part of my history sometimes slips out in casual conversation, I'm met with surprised looks.

You should have seen the look on my eight-year-old's face, for example, when my husband told her I was married once before. I hadn't mentioned it because not only did I think she was too young to understand, but, well, it was none of her business. Since the time I was pregnant I've endured the "just wait" commentary from practically every parent I know with older children who assure me there will come a time when my daughters believe I'm stupid, embarrassing and a complete loser. So, I suppose I didn't want to be labeled a loser before my time—or before *their* time as teenagers. I intended to instruct them on the subject of the disastrous first marriage and how to avoid it, but planned to wait until they had their first set of permanent teeth to do it.

But kids are learning everything earlier these days.

I usually like to shrug off the subject of my DFM by saying, "hey, you win some, you lose some." My divorced cousin said that to me after I disclosed my failure at a family gathering. "You win some, you lose some," she said as easily as she might say something like, "it's a lovely day." I liked the sound of it and tucked the saying into my back pocket. With the win-some/lose-some philosophy and because there weren't any children involved, it was fairly easy to cast aside the failure and move on.

Now that I'm the mother of two daughters—in other words, there *are* children involved in my life—I feel even more strongly that they should wait until they're say, comfortably past the "identity years," whatever those years may be on the age scale, (perhaps thirty?) before getting married. I cry mother-of-the-bride tears just thinking of the day they might bring home THE boy, and hope they won't believe they're too in love and above the statistics of potential disastrous first marriages to not take heed of their mother's experience.

Whenever I use the phrase "my first husband" I feel the urge to mime a drag from an imaginary cigarette holder and talk like Bette Davis. So, picture me that way as I relate the following. After my first husband (inhale) and I filed the divorce papers, we managed to stay apart for two years. (Exhale). There was virtually no contact, no planned or accidental meetings. Part of the time we lived in different towns and even different states. In that time I stopped being mad at him for blaming me for everything, especially after I met with his mother, who told me she understood he was probably a lousy husband because he had no example set for him by his father, her first husband. "You deserve to have everything in a marriage that you *think* you deserve," she said while I devoured tea and scones and she smoked cigarettes. "And don't ever settle for less or let anyone tell you that you should."

I took her advice to heart and loved her for saying this, which is something I desperately needed to hear. It was much more useful than my own mother's advice, which came when I first disclosed there were troubles with the young marriage. "Are you making your bed everyday, dear?" she asked sweetly. I still want to throw up whenever I think of her saying that to me. Especially because I believed her. I believed that each day it was my responsibility to gather the crinkled wads of sheets from the corners of our horribly uncomfortable waterbed with the makeshift two-by-six frame, and pull them smooth over the pillows. And it was my responsibility to do all the grocery shopping, all the cooking, all the vacuuming and dusting, take out all the garbage, collect, pay and manage all the bills as well as the checking account and the tax returns, and even mow the stupid patch of lawn outside our little rented in-law apartment. It was my responsibility to fend for myself in a big city where I knew very few people while he was on the golf course with his buddies or riding his precious bicycle one hundred miles each weekend. Or happily wait for him to complete his daily routine of fifty pushups, sit-ups and pull-ups before we went to a dinner party or a concert, which always made us late. I had to accept the fact that he chose not to shower over the weekend, and then take care of his dirty laundry, which was usually scattered throughout the apartment. While the other married women I worked with often met their husbands for lunch, I either walked to the Macy's at Union Square to buy new sheets on sale during the White Flower Days, or ate from a brown paper bag at my desk while my husband went to the YMCA and then ran miles along the Embarcadero each day. I started running with him out of self-defense until I developed asthma from living in a place where molds and allergens never froze. When it got the best of me and I had to stop and catch my breath—or sometimes lay on the ground and gasp for air—I endured his criticism. "You're just out of shape and weak, Michele." I felt like I was married to a lion tamer, who might crack the whip on my back at any time and beat me into shape.

And then one night, he did beat me. He did a good job of it, too. He administered a permanent injury that I only have to look in the mirror, smile and see a capped front tooth to remember the feeling of having my face thrust into a car door on a dark, rainy night. I can see the lightening flash behind my eyes, hear the chink of my perfect tooth as it hit the pavement and taste the bitterness of the blood that filled my mouth as the skin on my nose and mouth tore open. And I remember the devastating emotion of believing I deserved it. That it was, like everything else that had gone wrong, entirely my fault.

The physical abuse was something new that night, but the psychological abuses had lurked in the sharp corners of our relationship for a very long time. They were in a place where no one saw them. Not even me.

Eventually I learned what was going on through sessions with a good shrink. My doctor must have been a Freudian because we spent a lot of time talking about my father and the theory that many girls grow up to marry men just like their fathers. In my first husband, I chose a man who I felt merited my esteem because he constantly confirmed the worst opinions I had of myself. And those opinions formed during the days spent under the same roof as my dear old dad.

My father wasn't particularly physically abusive—although I do remember growing up in a "spare the rod, spoil the child" age and having my bottom spanked on many occasions. Mostly my mother took responsibility for lame spankings with a paddle on which one of my older sisters wrote in a navy blue crayon "Slap 'em Good, Ma!" We'd cringe any time a parting gift from a birthday party included one of those wooden paddles with a thin piece of elastic string and red rubber ball stapled to it. They were usually good for two or three sessions of the ball slapping game before the staple gave way and only left behind another spanking mechanism for "Ma." My mother was so tiny that there wasn't much wallop to her punishment. It wasn't long before I laughed at her whenever she threatened me with the Slap 'em good, Ma paddle. But that's when my father took over.

My dad liked to go for the nose. He had a mean streak, which reared its ugly head in the form of an index finger he used to thwack my nose whenever he didn't like the tone of my voice. Sometimes he even administered a vicious thwack when I spoke too loudly on the telephone. Those nasty thwacks shut me up in a hurry and made my eyes fill with tears.

My earliest memories—whether my family believes I was old enough to remember or not—were of the poem about the girl with the girl in the middle of her forehead, which was recited to me when I was a toddler with a glorious head full of strawberry curls. "When she was good she was very, very good. But when she was bad she was HORRID!" I grew up believing that I was a rotten kid with a father who didn't recognize my talents or contributions to the family. Although today he is supportive, loving and kind, when I was in high school, I can't remember one word of encouragement.

I was gifted athletically, performed with the dance troupe, wrote for the newspaper, had a zillion friends and at least when the braces were removed from my teeth, I was high school hot shit. But as my dad became mired in an alcohol and Valium haze of middle-aged depression, he rarely spoke to me unless it was to criticize. In the cloudy mirrors that were once his light blue eyes—my eyes—I wasn't hot shit anything. More like just plain shit.

I think this is why my mother became my champion. She recognized her husband's disdain for my personality and did her best to make up for it by becoming my best friend and confidant. During high school and college my mother and I were very close. She wrote letters to me every day and I knew I had her undying support. But she still had her beliefs and her agenda for raising children, which wasn't lost on me completely.

Devout Catholics, my parents put pressure on the subject of marriage-before-sex and actually helped supplement my meager student job income during my junior year when I threatened to move in with my boyfriend and share his room because I couldn't afford to pay rent that year. "You stay a virgin until you get married," my dad said to me one day over the phone. (Of course he had no idea that I had given up my virginity five minutes after I left home.) So, I kept my mouth closed around my guilt, aware my mother knew the truth. I was flabbergasted that he offered advice and appalled that he was so completely out of touch with my life. As far as I was concerned his opportunity to give advice sailed away with the virginity ship. I had a new man in my life to take over where Daddy left off and at age twenty-two, I was another victim of white lace dreams gone nightmare.

On the September day when my father happily escorted his tall, twenty-two year old foul-mouthed and disrespectful daughter down the aisle of that tiny church in Tiff, Missouri, he pecked me on the cheek, chirped "Goodbye!" and handed me over as if to say to his new son-in-law, "she's your problem now."

"Goodbye?" I asked with a dropped jaw. "That's it?"

That was another clue for me to RUN! But again, I didn't have the courage. I went through the ceremony and bonded myself to a man—a boy, really—who I had failed to recognize was a clone of my father, who continually heaped an equal amount of you're-nothing-more-than-shit commentary in my general direction. But the Freudian therapist insisted that the reason I married this man was because he made me "comfortable." Wearing the label of "rotten kid" was as comfortable as a favorite tee-shirt for me, and it was natural for me to be drawn to it. I found all kinds of ways to be a bad wife and within three months of uttering my hollow vows, I found someone else. (Someone who was the complete opposite of my husband.) But I couldn't live with the guilt brought on by the role of a sneaky, adulterous wife. So, I admitted my sin and watched the color drain from my husband's face.

Naturally, from that point forward things only got worse. But I was comfortable being the bad girl and, of course, accepted that everything was my fault. I begged him to keep me, tolerated his neglect as my penance and stayed with him for a year after he bashed in my face.

The Things I Wish I'd Said

I kept hearing my mother's voice: "Are you making your bed each day, dear?"

Yeah, I made it, Mom. I made it, laid in it and was miserable.

Finally, I grew tired of being the naughty girl—the girl with the godforsaken curl in the middle of her forehead—one Christmas eve when I came home early from work with grocery bags full and ready to prepare the figgie pudding for not only my husband, but his smelly younger brother and lazy girlfriend who showed up on our doorstep weeks before, sick after an aborted attempt to bicycle and camp throughout the Golden state during the rainy season. While they had spent the previous week with their unwashed bodies and dirty clothing sprawled all over our apartment, with the windows closed and the shades drawn, on Christmas Eve everyone was gone. Apparently they all went out to find their own figgie pudding at a pizza parlor in Berkeley and finally came home after nine o'clock with a rented VCR and a bunch of action films. By this time I had knocked over the Christmas tree in a fit of rage and had torn my clothes from their hangers in our tiny closet.

My punishment had gone on long enough. It was time to forgive myself and get out of that farcical marriage.

Like a New Year's resolution, in January I moved to a new apartment. The stinky brother and equally stinky girlfriend helped move my furniture, while my soon-to-be-ex-husband stood idly by without a word. Not even a peck on the cheek or a curt "goodbye."

The pool lady said that since there's a child involved in her pending divorce, the state of Arizona requires them to take a class about what it will mean for the children.

"They mentioned that one in two marriages ends in divorce," she said. "I think we knew going in we had a fifty-fifty chance of making it. But they had the nerve to tell us that seventy-five percent of second marriages fail," she said. "How's that for taking hope out of the future?"

I wished I could tell her what she clearly wanted to hear. I wanted to assure her that the second time down the aisle, we veteran brides walked with off-white experience and knowledge rather than pure-white hope, virginity and naïveté. But I knew my situation was different than hers. I didn't have children, and therefore stepchildren, to complicate the success of my second marriage. I've seen these custody complications up close and know they can take a terrible toll on second marriages.

Even without kids in the mix, when I took the plunge the second time around I was trembling with fright. I held my father's arm as he escorted me down the makeshift aisle of the yacht *California Spirit's* lower deck, feeling more like I was about to walk the plank and be fed to whatever creatures lurked in San Francisco Bay rather than onto the happy threshold of my new life. I was so curious as to what my dad would say to me the second time he "gave me away." Would he take advantage of the opportunity to improve on his curt "goodbye" nine years earlier?

I sat in the bow of the ship for the first part of the wedding day voyage. The cruise director said I shouldn't make my official appearance until we arrived at the cove near Angel Island, which is a calm spot on San Francisco Bay and a place where the captain could give up the helm and perform the ceremony. When the taped new age "water music" began and I made my way into the packed galley, I was grateful to have my tall and sturdy father to hold me up. I had entertained the option of walking alone given my first experience with his escort services, but I'm so glad he was with me. This time he gave me a warm kiss and drew me close. In my ear he said in a low voice, "get it right this time."

I'm happy to say I've taken my father's advice. Every day since that walk, along with my loving and wonderful husband, I believe I'm getting it right. Would this be the case if I hadn't experienced the disastrous first marriage? Would I have recognized the good without getting such a bitter mouthful of the bad?

I guess I'll never know. But my hope for my daughters is that they're fully aware of the potential for a DFM and that they will avoid it like the white lace plague.

And In This Corner . . .

March 3, 1992

When people learn that I write a column, very often they suggest topics for me to broach. Last week I not only got a suggestion, I had a request.

"Did you write about the Mike Tyson rape trial yet?" this occasional reader asked. When I told him I hadn't, he suggested this topic would make for interesting reading. He also wanted to know my opinion. So here it is.

I'm not a psychic and I'm hesitant to take credit for successful predictions without any formal declaration or proof. But on the high-society, high profile rape case circuit, I'm two-for-two in the verdict-prediction department.

Just as my gut feeling was that William Kennedy Smith would be pronounced not guilty in his rape trial months earlier, I predicted that former heavyweight boxing champion Mike Tyson would go down. These predictions were made before the cases were tried. Without hearing the evidence, I passed judgment.

My reasoning was basic. Willie Smith is a Kennedy. He's white. He's wealthy. His (middle) name defines political muscle. Regardless of all the Kennedy-bashing going on in stand-up comedy routines across the country, this family is still American royalty.

It seems we the people have a protective instinct over the admirable Kennedy clan. And heck, if we convicted Willie, we might have to go back and get Teddy for Chappaquiddick or decide once and for all that Lee Harvey Oswald did not act alone. This would be too much for us.

The Things I Wish I'd Said

Political power like this knows no boundaries.

In another example that took place a few weeks before the Smith trial, we witnessed Clarence Thomas' appointment to the Supreme Court. His approval came about in spite of charges of sexual harassment brought forth by an intelligent, credible accuser. Using the traditional, despicable defense that the victim, Anita Hill, was to be blamed for her predicament, the Senate Judiciary Committee did its best to discredit her. She and her charges were dismissed.

Clearly, when political muscle flexes, it wins. The same cannot be said for the muscle of a boxer.

Former heavyweight champion Mike Tyson represents the antithesis to Smith and power politics. In spite of the similarities in their rape cases, the only thing these defendants had in common was a high profile.

Until his conviction in an Indianapolis courtroom, Tyson was one of the highest paid thugs in America. His profession, boxing—which I prefer to call legalized aggravated assault—is sponsored by glitzy gambling casinos and promoted by the new age Dons: Donald Trump, who suggested that Tyson buy his way out of jail by donating proceeds from future fights to rape counseling centers in the state of Indiana, and Don King, a convicted killer who looks like a cartoon character who got scared.

These are people we love to hate. Even though we glorify these palookas for their money or for their super human ability to pummel another man to near death, we are right there to despise and condemn them when the opportunity arises.

Their flamboyance does not have to answer to the voters of this country. They act like they are above it all. And this includes, perhaps, the law. They'll get the best attorneys that money can buy to defend their cases, but if they lose, it is not an American tragedy.

The sport of boxing hones and glorifies masculinity. It can turn a derelict like Tyson, who was discovered at the age of thirteen at a school for juvenile delinquents in upstate New York, into a multimillionaire, rewarded only for his ability to inflict injury.

That the twenty-five-year-old Tyson was accused and convicted of committing rape should surprise no one. Rape is, after all, the supreme macho gesture. And with Tyson's reputation for being emotionally unstable and volatile, many of his boxing peers predicted that he'd either end up dead or in jail at a very young age.

The thing we don't seem to realize as a society is that it doesn't necessarily take a modern day gladiator to commit the violent crime of rape.

Our decisions may be split, but they're made before the trials even begin.

It Pay$ to Be Bad

I had barely finished retyping this column from the folded, yellowing newspaper clipping when I heard a commercial on TV advertise the noon news. "It looks like Mike Tyson may be in trouble again," recited the anchorwoman. "This time it's in Arizona and if you tune in at noon, we'll tell you all about it."

Mike Tyson has been "in trouble" so many times in the past ten years that it has become as mundane as Bill Clinton making a public appearance, Julia Roberts winning an award or Stephen King publishing a scary story. As if Tyson's infamous 1997 biting episode, when he decided to have Evander Holyfield's ear as a snack during a bout, weren't enough to keep him tucked away in the "News of the Weird" column for life, we continually have our own news-hungry ears raped by the escapades of this thug.

That day an exotic dancer in Phoenix claimed Tyson punched her. His lawyer denied the charges. Prior to that a stripper in Las Vegas claimed Tyson assaulted her. His response to these slips into psychosis is that he "has to be evil in order to earn a living." And in a way he's right because his antics continue receiving full media coverage.

In spite of all this, Tyson still claims to be a humble fellow.

Obviously this fellow never learned how to use a dictionary because he doesn't know the meaning of the word "humble." He has never apologized for being the convicted rapist of the eighteen-year old beauty queen Desiree Washington and said publicly that it was her fault. He also hasn't apologized for biting Holyfield. I suppose that was Holyfield's fault, too. Perhaps his ears just looked too delicious.

Publicizing an upcoming bout with fellow convicted felon, Clifford "the Black Rhino" Etienne, who did ten years for armed robbery, he told the media he was "tired of being stupid." (We're tired of it, too.) When the reporters said something about it being the "Jailhouse Bout," Tyson still dismissed the rape charge and professed he "didn't do it." And then his opponent leaned into the microphone and said with a rhino's low grumble, "Yeah, but I *did!*"

Boxing attracts criminals the way the stock market attracts gamblers. Another criminal stepping into the ring was the notorious spark plug on skates, Tonya Harding, who claimed professional boxing was her new career. Banned for life from the United States Figure Skating Association because of the assault on fellow skater Nancy Kerrigan, this thirty-two year old former Olympic athlete discovered boxing after her attempt at a singing career failed and when she had the opportunity to punch out Bill Clinton's nemesis, Paula Jones, on Fox TV's "Celebrity Boxing." Harding said she liked boxing because it allowed her to let out "pent up anger" against her opponent. "I feel sorry for the girl who steps in the ring with me," she said. Anyone who witnessed the pained face of Nancy Kerrigan after she took a blow to the knee with an iron pipe at the 1994 National Figure Skating Championships (*"WHY?"*) knew how sorry *she* was to have stepped in the rink with the likes of Tonya Harding.

Ring or rink, it's all just plain rank.

Since the Tyson and Smith rape trials, there have been many notorious celebrity trials including the mother of all celebrity trials, the O.J. Simpson murder trial, which penetrated the airwaves for 133 days. I didn't predict the outcome of that trial and didn't watch the evidence unfold on television; but I, along with ninety-one percent of all those watching television that day, tuned in for the verdict.

My friends and I discussed O.J. Simpson many years before the murders of Nicole Brown Simpson and Ronald Goldman put him on trial. His persona penetrated the streets of white suburbia during his days as a Heismann Trophy-winning running back for USC and then as a superstar for the Buffalo Bills. We had footballs with his reproduced signature and pretended to be him during street games, while trying to get past every boy in our Chicago Bears-crazed neighborhood on defense pretending to be "Dick Butkus." We hurdled furniture saying his name because of his commercials for the Hertz Rental Car Company, and again said his name any time we saw someone running through an airport.

During this era I remember a curbside discussion about O.J. Simpson with a group of neighborhood kids, half who went to the Catholic school and half to the public school across the street. After the games of football or foursquare or a version of Capture the Flag we played called "Relievio," where we all meshed together to form the teams, we could be easily divided according to our schools. Our "gangs" were the Catholics versus the Publics. I was a Catholic. And in 1969 we Catholics were introduced to the concept of "busing," which meant inner city black students would soon attend our lilywhite schools. I didn't think bussing would have much affect on me and had no problem with the idea. I was in fourth grade and didn't know much about, well, anything, but even less about race relations. My sister, however, a senior in high school, rode the Burlington Northern train to Chicago each afternoon as part of the work program and met a girl named Janice. Janice was black.

Janice was like a folk hero in our house—the first black friend any of us had had—and she taught my sister all the latest new dances like the football and the push-and-pull, which she in turn taught us. My sister even accompanied Janice and some friends to see James Brown in concert, and I remember being sworn to secrecy on that one, as our father would have never allowed it. (Not that he knew who James Brown was, but associating with a "group of coloreds" for a night of "jungle music" would certainly be forbidden.) My sister and her friend taught us to use the term "black," instead of "colored," and we loved her bright, white smile and how she always touched us and said we were so cute.

The only other blacks we "knew" were The Temptations, Diana Ross and the Supremes, the Jackson Five and O.J. Simpson.

The Things I Wish I'd Said

O.J. Simpson transcended race. We white kids claimed him for ourselves.

As the busing discussion continued, some of the older kids, the seventh and eighth graders, made comments about having to "watch their backs" in the hallways or that they'd probably need to start carrying knives.

Then someone asked, "Would you ever kiss a black guy?" Most of the girls said something along the lines of "eeeeeoooowwww;" however, another girl gave the question greater definition.

"Okay, so you say you'd never kiss a black guy, but would you ever kiss O.J. Simpson?"

I would have definitely kissed O.J. Simpson. So would have most of the other girls in that group of Catholics and Publics. Because he was a proven football hero, and he *was* cute, we learned how to see beyond skin tone.

But on the day in 1995 when he was proclaimed "not guilty" for the murders of his ex-wife and her friend, race lines were once again drawn more clearly in that the African American community cheered and the white community hissed, as if to say, "We let him get too close and we forgot to watch our backs."

I think there's a predominant feeling in this country today, at least among the white community, that O.J. got away with murder. I don't think we can say he reaped any financial benefit due to the limelight of his murder trial, which had all the elements of a trashy novel, but if he did get away with murder, freedom is certainly a valuable stipend.

As kids playing touch football in the streets of suburbia, we not only learned to sort through (and hopefully discard) our inherited bigotry, we were also taught that crime doesn't pay. But the muckraking tabloid world we grew into has shown us a whole string of notorious celebrities who have certainly proved in an odd way, that it pays to be bad.

Role Model or Artist?

December 3, 1991

A friend of mine proclaimed in the early '80s that, for the rest of his life, he would most likely be hearing news of Michael Jackson.

This was shortly after the release of *Thriller*, which sold 38 million copies and was the first and only Michael Jackson album I ever bought. Then came the cosmetic changes he made to his face, news of the Beatles' songs to which he attained the rights, Elephant Man remains and the exotic animal collection.

My friend's proclamation was true.

And the recent release of Jackson's latest video, "Black or White," including the instant controversy surrounding it, proved him correct once again.

My friend and I are about the same age as Michael Jackson. We both remembered his debut with the Jackson 5 on *American Bandstand* back in 1969.

While he watched from another part of the country, I was watching television with one of my teenaged sisters, Debra, when Dick Clark introduced this new Motown sensation, The Jackson 5. They performed their first hit "I Want You Back," led by eleven year-old Michael.

We loved the music. It brought us to our feet. "Get in here and see this group," cried Debra to the rest of the family. "This little kid is singing about love and ooh, ooh baby!"

The Things I Wish I'd Said

It was the novelty of Michael's youth and his beautiful, high-pitched voice that made us listen. The dancing, done in perfect unison by the five Jackson brothers, was like nothing we had ever seen.

Even my oldest sister, Mary Beth, who worked in downtown Chicago and was always bringing home the latest dance steps liked what she saw in the Jackson 5. She went out and bought a purple suede vest with two feet of fringe because "it was just like Michael Jackson's."

Recently her ten year-old son, Brandon, wore this same vest for Halloween. Brandon, however, wasn't trying to be like Michael Jackson. Rockstar names like "Axl Rose" or generic terms like "hippie" were closer to his intentions. If he wanted to dress up like Michael Jackson today, it would require something more than a purple vest.

It would probably take plastic surgery.

I videotaped the television premier of Michael Jackson's "Black or White" by accident.

My husband, who was busy working in his garage that night, had asked me to record *The Simpsons*. Since this show had already started, I pushed the REC button rather than set the timer and then forgot to turn it off.

The next day everybody at work was buzzing about "Black or White." I remember hearing words like "incredible" and "cool." They said it appeared right after *The Simpsons* and that parts of it were shown later on the local news.

I went home, fast-forwarded through *The Simpsons* and watched the tape.

As always, Michael Jackson impressed me with his music and his dancing—especially the moonwalking. And the video-imaging technique known as "morphing," where people's faces transform into other people's faces blew me away. Then came the panther, the zipper and the window smashing—the part of the video that has now been cut.

Now, I must say that ever since the advent of HBO, not much on television surprises me anymore. But during this segment, my jaw dropped and my eyes popped. Wow.

164

Michele VanOrt Cozzens

It was just like the day I watched *American Bandstand* back in 1969. "Get in here and see this," I called to my husband.

At this point, I knew censorship was inevitable.

Michael Jackson stopped being only an artist years ago. Instead, like almost all of today's musicians and celebrities, he became an example. A role model.

And just like we expected kids to start talking in 2-Live Crew lyrics and exposing themselves in public like Pee Wee Herman, because of the Jackson video, we believed they'd go out and start smashing car windows.

We can't have role models who smash car windows.

In spite of the violence and sexual innuendo presented by Michael Jackson in "Black or White," it is still some of the best dancing I've ever seen. I'm not sure why he felt the need to grab his crotch so much or what any of the censored segment had to do with the message of his song about racial equality. But as an artist, he certainly has the right to express himself.

Some say he caused the controversy just for the attention.

Well, he got my attention. And, no doubt, he'll continue to get it for as long as I live.

A Pound of Flesh

Michael Jackson is, of course, still in the news. Today, however, we don't use the term "role model." We don't even use the term "artist." Guilty or not guilty of the latest charges against him, we use the term "pedophile." Since I published the above piece, he was cleared of the first round of sexual abuse allegations, then married and divorced Lisa Marie Presley and again married and divorced a woman who bore two, maybe three children for him—one of which he dangled over a balcony in Germany, and all of which might carry the name "Prince." Currently facing the serious charges of sexual abuse against a minor, we now know for certain that where Michael Jackson is concerned, the topic isn't even close to being about his music.

I recall virtually no response to my column questioning our society's choices of role models. All I can guess is that I wasn't "well-known" enough or widely read enough to have this futile commentary generate a reaction. I wish I'd asked readers who their role models were. Perhaps that would have generated a response. Perhaps not.

In our culture, no one cares what you have to say unless you're a celebrity. In other words, the only way to become a role model is to first be a professional athlete, a popular artist or a domestic diva. That's what gets you noticed and that's what makes the media sit up and listen. It makes book publishers issue hefty advances, editors reserve space in magazines and advertising agencies salivate at the prospect of selling more products through celebrity endorsements. It's why we see Peggy Fleming talk about her cholesterol and Dorothy Hammil tell us about how to soothe arthritis while she skates through a commercial. Since she inspired a whole generation of high school girls to cut their hair in a "Hammil wedge" and use Short and Sassy shampoo, she can probably coax them into using some drug to soothe their aches and pains in middle age.

As a singing youngster, I'm sure Michael Jackson couldn't wait to appear with his brothers on American Bandstand or have his broad nose and bright smile shine out on the cover of *Teen* or *Tiger Beat* magazines. Nowadays, however, I imagine him cringing behind his mask whenever his altered face is on the cover of anything.

All celebrity comes with a price and a warning. One cannot become a celebrity without seeking and achieving maximum exposure. Even the biggest movie stars have to whore themselves on press junkets on the eve of their big opening. And since the media is already interested in them, it's easy to get the gigs. It's just that the savvy questioners will no doubt turn from movie plot to personal life and expect the same neatly unfolding story line.

The very publicity they may seek to further their careers may easily backfire.

In other words, it's just as easy to attract negative attention, as it is positive attention. Look at Kobe Bryant. Do we think of him first as an NBA Basketball star or an accused rapist? And how about Martha Stewart? Lifestyle guru or convicted felon? How about former President Bill Clinton? With his shattered legacy I can only wonder who on earth believes he (or she) is perfect enough to run for President of the United States?

We love our celebrities, but it seems we love it even more when we can knock them of the very pedestals we built for them. We hold them to such high standards; elevating them to royalty status and watch with growing contempt as they name their children "Prince." With the god and goddess stature heaped upon them it becomes impossible to simply be human in the midst of such a heavenly aura.

I was on a trip recently with some of my girlfriends and they decided to play a practical joke on me that, as it developed a life of its own, became a joke out of control. I had my photograph taken thinking I might use it for my next book cover. It was a big mistake for reasons I'm still trying to sort out. Perhaps it was that little toe-dip into celebrity that comes with promoting a book that made my friends uncomfortable and triggered their need to put me in my place. They made countless copies of the photo, defaced most of them and papered the public hallways, the private rooms we rented, used them as placemats and labels on wine bottles. At first it was funny. They were quite clever in their project and in their methods of distracting and surprising me. As I laughed—taking my expected role as the butt of the joke—they laughed with me and called me a good sport.

But the joke wouldn't die and I grew tired of being the center of attention. While they expected me to be flattered, expected me to bask in the limelight given my previous efforts to attain publicity for book sales, what they didn't understand is the terrible burden of facing negative attention versus positive attention.

It gave me a much better appreciation for what artists go through to promote their work and earn their livings, and was another lesson in being prepared to face what comes when putting oneself out there. It's why I'll always believe that a person—famous or unknown—is innocent until proven guilty. And why I'm very careful in choosing who I want my role models to be.

I don't expect perfection of myself. I expect it even less in others.

The Things I Wish I'd Said

The only role model I want to be is the one I took on with the job of motherhood. And as I scratch and crawl my way towards the (lime) light trying to get my work read and reviewed, I want to raise my hand in a stop position if I give anyone the idea that I intend elevate myself to the status of role model. If I inspire you to write your memories and impressions and get your own book published, that's great. But if I start dancing on stage or telling you what will cure your aches and pains, be afraid. Be *very* afraid.

I'm happy to teach my kindergartner to tie her shoes so she gets a jingle bell for Christmas from her teacher and I'll further teach both girls to floss, separate the whites and colors and turn off the oven when they're finished making cupcakes. I'll teach them to be kind and use their manners, to attend church and follow the dress code at school, even when it means wearing sleeves on a day when it's a hundred degrees. I'll teach them to send thank-you notes and use "indoor voices," eat all their food when they're invited to dinner and tell each guest at their birthday parties that they loved the gifts (as opposed to saying "I HATE Barbies" or I already HAVE that book!)

That should take care of most of my role model requirements. And in the meantime, I'll leave the medical advice to the doctors, and I'll certainly leave the moonwalking to our old friend, Michael Jackson—that is, if he can still do it after we take away his pound of flesh.

Chapter 4

Roots

Parents are the bones on which

children sharpen their teeth.

—Peter Ustinov, *Dear Me*

For Better or Worse

September 3, 1991

Yesterday my parents celebrated their 48th wedding anniversary. Whew! Considering that's my entire lifetime plus many, many more years, it's hard for me to fathom such an eternity. But believe it or not, if Mom and Dad were characters on The Love Boat, they might be cast as newlyweds. They are very much in love.

Now, I'm not suggesting that their entire marriage has been laced with flowers, candy and sweet nothings. Raising five baby boomers in a blue-collar suburb of Chicago (with two of them—myself and my younger sister—popping out when they were in their 40s) was no easy feat.

But they survived. And when I look at them today I can't help but frame them inside a storybook that begins with "Once upon a time" and ends with, of course, "happily every after."

Cupid has been good to Tom and Kay.

Catherine Ann Kernan, today known as Kay (and Na-Na Kay to her nine grandchildren), was born and raised in the Irish Catholic community of Melrose, Massachusetts. Her father was a carpenter, her mother a piano teacher. She was called Katie by her friends and "Pretty Kitty Kernan" by the corner grocer.

Katie was an "A" student, and the way I understand it, had she not had to work to help support her mother (who was widowed during the Depression), she very well might have joined the convent.

171

But then came World War II and with it, a blond-haired, blue-eyed Coast Guard sailor from Chicago named Tom, who looked to her like Van Johnson.

"At first I didn't like him," I've heard my mom say about Dad, "because he couldn't dance. And at that time, dancing was the thing to do."

But somehow the long-legged sailor persisted and managed to get an invitation to Kay's house for dinner. And from that event comes a story repeated quite often at the VanOrt family dinner table. It seems the menu that evening included a spinach dish. When it was offered to Tom by his future mother-in-law his response was a turned-up lip. "Spinach!" he scoffed. "I'm not Popeye. I *hate* spinach."

Happily, however, Tom's more charming characteristics prevailed, and he did learn to dance. In fact one of his claims to fame is that he actually danced with Lana Turner one evening at a club in New York City.

In 1943 Tom and Kay decided they would marry. Yet since the war was in full swing and Tom continued his convoys across the Atlantic, it was difficult to set a wedding date. "The next time I'm in port," he said, "we'll get married." It could have been weeks, months … Perhaps he would never come back.

But the time passed quickly. And with only a day or two's notice, Pretty Kitty Kernan had to scramble to get a wedding planned. She borrowed dresses from her recently wed neighbor, the local bake shop whipped up a cake, Tom's mother flew in from Chicago, and on a Thursday morning they took the vows that would carry them through the next several decades.

Their honeymoon lasted years as Kay traveled with him from port to port. Eventually she moved far and forever away from her mother and only sister to be with Tom's family in Chicago. Her mother passed away shortly thereafter, and her sister, a severe asthmatic, died a few years after that.

After suffering the stillbirth of their first child and fearful that they might never have children, their first baby, Mary Beth, was born in 1951.

• • •

Today while their kids are spread out in different states, Tom and Kay live in the foothills of the Missouri Ozarks or where I like to refer to as "On Golden Pond." They've got a ski boat that Dad steers while Mom slalom skies around and around the small lake. They drive their golf cart to the nearby links and then later cruise around the red dirt roads on a little Honda mini-bike, waving to their friends in the community as they pass by.

My parents, no matter where they are, still go to Mass every Sunday, and I know they pray for all of us, as well as give thanks for their many blessings. They've been a wonderful example.

The thing I admire most about their marriage, however, is that they are truly each other's best friend. And obvious to anyone, each other's biggest fan.

Happy Anniversary Mom and Dad.

Until Death Us Do Part

Today my dad lives alone. Whether or not he still keeps my mother's blue, Michigan ball cap on top of her pillow every night, I don't know. But he signs her name to the occasional letter he writes ("Love from Dad and Mom,") and visits her gravesite each day. It's a gravesite he had never planned to see.

He never planned to see a gravesite since my mother intended to donate her body to science. Both my parents made the decision to be cadavers when my sister was in medical school. Cadavers are to med-schools what naked models are to art schools and apparently, there's a shortage. The international standard for gross anatomy students assigned to dissect a human body is four students per cadaver. (In China where cadaver donation has only recently been legalized, twelve students must crowd around a body.) I don't know if my sister sent our parents paperwork on the subject the way my kids bring home requests for donations of cookies for bake sales or if my mother read something about the cadaver shortage on her own and made this decision; however, both parents were on board the cadaver donation train. They shared the official paperwork with me shortly after their decision and pointed to the section indicating "full body donations provide no remains."

"Now, we want you to make sure this happens," they said, trading words. (My parents always spoke about death as if they'd die together.) "We think your sister, Mary Beth, might have a problem with it."

"Why do you think that?" I asked, while the acrid odor of formalde-hyde suddenly filled my senses in the form of a memory from when I worked in the Life Sciences building in college. I lifted the paperwork to my nose, wondering if the pages had been dipped in that rank substance to preserve them for all time. I felt a sneeze coming on.

"Mary is emotional," said my mother.

And I'm not? I tried to act sophisticated and unfazed by the discussion, wanting to believe my parents had faith in my maturity level (a first) and could talk to me like a client talks to a lawyer about estate planning. But I did not want to visualize the death of my parents and wished to God they'd change the subject.

Ultimately, my mother didn't get to be a cadaver. She never had four Missouri medical students dissect her preserved corpse and address her as Mrs. VanOrt, spray her down, wrap her up and retag her toe over the course of a semester, and it had nothing to do with Mary Beth's or anyone's protests. After a massive stroke rendered her brain dead, her vital organs became more valuable than her cadaver and while her 80-year-old Irish liver went to Kansas City (or was it Nebraska?) her other vital organs were, we're told, put to very beneficial scientific use. Her desire to be useful was fulfilled and my father was given her remains. I don't think he ever allowed himself to think about the death of his wife, and therefore, he hadn't planned a gravesite. So, when the remains were suddenly bestowed upon him, he created a place to store them in a way that was distinctly his own.

The gravesite Tom made for Kay is both quaint and terribly pathetic at the same time. The marker is constructed with two-by-fours of treated lumber forming a cross, and is held together by recycled nails from his twenty-year-old deck project. (To know my father is to know that he is constantly working at rebuilding the deck surrounding his house.) Written in black marker—fading like disappearing ink since the day he wrote on the wood—on the left side is "Kay, 1919-1999." The right side of the cross has his name, "Tom, 1920 – ". I suppose he believes we'll bury his remains there, too, in the backyard under his dilapidated deck.

I think it might be up to me to ask him if he still wants his body donated to science or if he would rather go the same route as Mom and donate his remaining vital organs. His corneas would make a lovely gift.

When the time comes I don't know what we'll do, because I'm too emotional to think about it right now. But I know it's important that Tom and Kay always remain together.

True As a Level. Right as a Rule.

October 22, 1991

Wrong as a misspelled word. That's what I was in a recent column, "For better or for worse," a tribute to my parents on their 48th wedding anniversary. In reference to my maternal grandparents, whom I never knew, I said that grandma was a piano teacher (true) and grandpa was a carpenter. Untrue. I don't know why I thought he was a carpenter. Perhaps it had something to do with the John Prine tune "Grandpa Was a Carpenter," which was running through my head the day I wrote that column.

My uncertainty about grandpa's occupation was of concern before the piece was published. I attempted to check this fact with two of my sisters, Gayle and Mary Beth, who both said, "Uh, I think he was a carpenter. But I'm not sure. You know, Mom doesn't talk about her parents very much."

Gayle mentioned something about a grocery store, but I discarded it because I had never heard anything about a store. I didn't call my parents to check facts because I wanted the piece to be a surprise.

It was a surprise, all right.

Soon after receiving it, my mother wrote me a letter in which she set straight the story of her father's occupation. The following is an excerpt:

"My dad would be surprised to be called a 'carpenter.' He was a farmer. True he didn't have a big farm—just a vegetable garden. He and my mother had a little grocery store. During the day my dad peddled groceries and delivered orders while my mother tended store. He also worked as a shoe-cutter in Lynn, Massachusetts. Lynn was a big shoe-manufacturing center. Later he worked in the village with the road crew.

"My dad loved the land and growing vegetables and flowers. When business was bad and they gave up the store, he continued to grow a garden. It was his hobby. That and reading seed catalogues and Zane Gray stories. But he was born a farmer and he died a farmer."

So, grandpa was a farmer. Of this, now, I am absolutely sure. I can now paint a clearer picture of him in my mind where he has black, curly hair and sepia-toned skin—the kind you see in old photographs. He wears suspenders and has a faded pair of gloves stuffed loosely into his breast pocket. A small gardener's spade is in his hand. His eyes, I don't know, perhaps they are bluish-green like my mother's.

But yet, I cannot hear his voice. I cannot visualize his walk. Did he know how to throw a baseball? What kind of games did he play with his daughters? Was he a loving husband? Did he have many friends?

There is so much I don't know about my family's history.

Except for my father's mother, Florence, all my grandparents had passed away before my birth. And then, unfortunately, my grandmother died when I was very young and I never had the opportunity to really know her.

Having been born to a couple in their forties, my birth expanded a generation beyond the idealistic Ozzie and Harriet stuff—where people were sure of their roles—and into the confusion of the Vietnam War era, the women's movement and Watergate. I often feel that I was born too late. Too late for what, I'm not sure. I knew I was missing something.

During my senior year of college, I was assigned a term paper for a Journalism History course. For it I needed to interview one parent and one grandparent to uncover my own journalistic roots.

Knowing that he helped to support his family during the Depression with a newspaper delivery route, I chose to interview my father; but I was at a loss for a grandparent and on the verge of a panic attack.

To the rescue came an old man, in his late 70s at the time, named Marvin Spears. He was a lively little man with a head full of white hair and twinkling eyes. He was a talented painter, an inspiration to other aspiring artists in the retirement community where he lived. Upon my parents' request, he agreed to be my term paper grandfather.

I saw him only a couple times during the next few years—which were the last few years of his life—and I always greeted him by saying: "Hi-ya Gramps!" Marvin made me feel the way I always imaged a grandpa would make me feel. And that was very special.

Generation Span

As my parents before me, I have continued the wide generation gap in our family and have helped turn it from a gap into a span about as long as the Golden Gate Bridge. Today my father is eighty-four years old, and he is the only remaining grandparent my children have. While he will always be my daddy and I can still picture him without white hair or the slow limp he exhibits when he walks across the room, to my kids he's as old as Father Time.

I'm not sure either of my children could say what their Pop-Pop did for a living before retirement. Actually, I'm not sure they understand what it means to earn a living or that adults have additional roles outside of the walls of their homes.

When I wrote the above piece, I wrote through the eyes of a child. I felt that my parents belonged to me. I believed their personal histories were my domain and I had a right as their progeny to know the facts. Just as the two-year-old's mine-mine-mine mantra rings something like: "What's mine is mine; what's yours' is mine; what's my mommy's is mine;" even as a thirty-something woman, I still wanted my mommy's history to be mine. But it wasn't.

About a year before my first child was born, I went to Boston with my three sisters to spend an October weekend exploring a chapter in my mother's history. Our family portrait of Boston was colored with romance. And we all wanted a piece of it during that weekend. One sister, Debra, had a conference there and popped for a suite at the posh Plaza hotel, which is where my parents spent their wedding night in 1943. They met in this city during the War, when the tall and lean Chicago-boy was in port and the small, dark haired Irish lass was out with her sister and her friend looking for a dance.

Boston did not disappoint. We toured the old North Church and imagined the Midnight Ride of Paul Revere. We drank beer at Cheers and yelled "Norm" at every fat guy we saw. We strolled around Harvard Yard pretending to be intellectuals and later ate far too much lobster and jumped on Debra the next morning to see if her face broke out in "bolts," as she called the zits that usually showed up after eating shellfish.

On Saturday we took the T from downtown north to the small town of Melrose, where my mother was born. We visited the charming St. Mary's church and school, where our mother was an honor student from first grade through high school. And from the corner sidewalk, snapped photos as we imagined our gorgeous parents stepping out into the midweek sunlight after the ceremony, which our mother only had three days to plan when she learned her intended would be in port. From there we walked down the street and sat on the steps of the ochre saltbox house on Grove Street, a large and well-tended home where our mother spent her girlhood. Mom's best friend and our tour guide, Muriel, snapped our picture.

"So this is where Mom, her sister and parents lived," I said.

"It's where your mother, aunt and grandmother lived," said Muriel. "Your grandfather lived over in Lynn."

Four necks snapped as we shot surprised expressions at our mother's friend. In unison we all said, "huh?"

"Did I say something wrong?" asked Muriel covering her mouth. "You girls didn't know this?"

"We know very little about our mother's family," I said. "I wrote a column once saying her father was a carpenter and Mom was quick to correct me by saying he was a farmer."

"Is that all she told you?" Muriel asked with a raised eyebrow. "Lynn, Lynn, the city of sin. You never go out the way you came in."

All four sisters were at a loss. None of us could step up as the favorite daughter and divulge a shared confidence. (And our mother went to her grave without passing on the true story of her parent's separation.) For a family of devout Catholics, I suppose such a thing was simply unspeakable. I tried to ask her about it shortly after our Boston escapade, but she stiffened and told me she didn't want to talk about it. Her tone was so serious that I never dared to bring it up again.

It was that day when I learned that everything belonging to mommy was *not* mine.

And so today I write through the eyes of a mother as well as a child. I now see from both sides—eyes in the back of my head, as I tell my kids.

Through my children's eyes I see love, admiration and respect. It's a gift our children give us before they are remotely aware of what these terms mean. (Everyone warns me that this will change and I'm not counting the days.)

Before my children came along, I focused on the unconditional love shown to me through my dogs, who never failed to get up, wag a tail and greet me with a pink tongue dangling from a canine smile. But now this same excited greeting meets me each day at the bus stop in the form of a braided kindergartener who breaks into a run when she sees me, while she reaches into her Lisa Frank backpack to pull out everything she's made for me at school that day. If I let her, I'm sure she'd lick my face.

My second grader still lights up when I walk into the room, but the bulb isn't as bright as it used to be. She does, however, tend to follow me around the house like a duckling swimming behind its mother and constantly asks me questions that start with a two-syllable "Mo-om?" She begins each sentence this way. I beg her to just ask the question or make the statement without the introductory "Mo-om?"

Sometimes it's "But Mom . . ." And that's even worse because it prompts me to utter one of those mother statements like, "But nothing. Just do as I SAY!" and makes me realize that sooner or later, we all become our mothers.

The big difference between my mother and me is that my kids will have access to every detail of my life. One can only wonder if they'll have any interest.

Wherever Green Is Worn

March 17, 1992

When I was growing up in suburban Chicago, race was not a big issue for my classmates and me. Aside from the years 1969-71 when the Chicago Archdiocese bused in a handful of black students to our school, we were all white kids. And we were Catholic.

Just by looking at us it was hard to see any differences. Some of us were blonde, some brunette. There were lots of redheads. We were, after all, heavily Irish.

With a few exceptions, there was an even mixture of Irish, Italian and Polish descendents with names like McPhillips, Capilupo and Koslowski.

Still, the question, "What's your nationality?" was asked more often than anything else. It was our adolescent prelude to "What's your major?" and "What do you do for a living?" At the time, nationality was all we had to call our own.

It was during these years at Catholic school that I learned to celebrate St. Patrick's Day. March 17th was a banner day. We wore uniforms, but under those scratchy wool jumpers we put on white blouses with green trim, wore green socks and had green ribbons streaming from our pigtails. Our moms included shamrock cookies in our brown-bag lunches, and sometimes the nuns let us watch Mayor Daly lead the city of Chicago's St. Patrick's Day parade on television. Every year they dyed the Chicago River green. It was something to see—no matter what your nationality.

The Things I Wish I'd Said

Most of the Polish and Italian kids got into the green of things on this day and they were encouraged to believe that "everyone is Irish on St. Patrick's Day." But as we started to grow up a little bit, several of the Italian kids started protesting this glorification of one nationality.

They, I remember, deliberately wore orange or red instead of green on the 17th, and then two days later on March 19th, the feast day of St. Joseph, they noisily celebrated their Italian heritage.

The nationality clash never went beyond those two days. We didn't have gang wars; we didn't choose sides or permanent colors. On March 20th, we all melted right back into the same big, Catholic pot.

The Catholic school I attended was known as St. Louise de Marillac. To this day I don't know where Marillac is or was, but I believe the elementary school is still standing in La Grange Park, Illinois.

I went there from the first through fifth grades. After fifth grade, I, along with my younger sister, was transferred to the public school across the street from St. Louise. This was a radical move for my parents—especially for my mother who considered parochial education an absolute requirement for her children. But I wanted desperately to play volleyball, and the Catholic schools did not yet have sports programs for girls—unless you counted cheerleading.

I also wanted to trade in my clarinet for an oboe, and St. Louise did not supply instruments either. So, I gave up a superior education on account of a funny-sounding instrument that I could never quite master. But with God as my witness, I was a dynamite volleyball player. (My sister, who was reluctant to transfer because she didn't want to leave her friends, was easily motivated once she learned she didn't have to wear a uniform at the public school.)

Our new classmates—kids we once referred to as "publics"—were of the same homogeneous variety as the Catholic school, and St. Patrick's Day was still celebrated. On this day everyone sported a wee bit of green clothing or wore a big button reading "Kiss me, I'm Irish." In the sixth through eighth grades, kissing was a bigger deal than St. Patrick's Day could ever be.

We'd trade in our nationality for a game of "Spin the Bottle" any day of the week.

Each March my Irish mother keeps the spirit of St. Patrick's Day in my life. She never fails to send a note with a shamrock sticker and wishes me good luck. She reminds me to wear green and sometimes encloses a green ribbon. I usually tied this ribbon to my dog's collar. Her name was Gaelic, Shonah, so this made sense to me. Shonah died last May, however. So it looks like this year I'll have to wear that green ribbon myself.

I always did look good in green.

Irish Pride

My first daughter was born about a week before St. Patrick's Day in 1995. That year my mother sent a green ribbon to her, which I promptly stuck to her head (she didn't yet have hair, and didn't actually get any until she was about a year old), and dressed her in a pale green "onesie." Then I snapped her picture and it scared the leprechaun right out of my husband.

"You're not going to be one of those moms who dresses up her kids in funny costumes for the holidays, are you?" he asked. Up until that point I hadn't given much thought to what kind of mom I intended to be other than one who breastfed in public without a care. Let it be known that when I still had complete power over dressing my children, I didn't treat them like they were dolls and actually cursed myself for not having spent more time as a child dressing and undressing dolls. Perhaps I would have been more skilled at getting my fingers around tiny buttons and better at snapping the three-thousand snaps going up and around giant diapers than I was when clothing my living, breathing babies. They have been known to sport the occasional baby Santa Claus suit at Christmas and on Halloween the whole family dresses up to join the neighborhood for trick-or-treat. But for the most part I don't turn them into holiday decorations.

On St. Patrick's Day, however, I do lay out the green. Part of it is habit. And the other part is to honor my mother. My husband is of Irish heritage as well and now that my children have been to Ireland, I think they can appreciate what this means.

So can I.

Over Christmas, 2001, my sister-in-law planned a trip to Dublin for all of us. Undeniably an expert on Irish history and culture, she has visited this country too many times to count. She has led many student groups to the Emerald Isle and also writes regular articles regarding her travels for the *New York Times*. She was the perfect tour guide during our four-day stint in and around Dublin, and I had never seen her happier. "Thank you for coming to *my* country," she said.

If one spends any time in Ireland, I dare say it's impossible to fly away and not have learned something about Irish history. Her citizens seem to live and breathe it. Each taxi driver we encountered acted as a tour guide ("over there is where they made the film *The Commitments*") and each tour guide like a college professor giving names and dates of incarcerations, marriages and executions as though speaking of their own family members.

Ever the college professor herself, my sister-in-law suggested we view two movies before our trip, in order for us to better understand some of the sites on our travel itinerary. Like a dutiful student, I drove to Blockbuster and rented *Michael Collins* and *In The Name of The Father* the day I received the "assignment." Since we were further instructed that everything in the country closed down on Christmas Day and we'd be on our own for entertainment after our meal that day, I wondered if she'd make us present our essay papers before we exchanged gifts.

The first place we visited in the city of Dublin was Kilmainham Gaol. (Gaol is pronounced, "jail" and now that I've been there I see this word in the crossword puzzles all the time). Kilmainham Gaol is a restored stone and steel structure, and is no longer an operating prison. It is a museum steeped in history and testament to Ireland's long struggle for independence from England. The focus of our tour guide, who recited an interminable litany of names and dates in a pleasant, lilting accent, was the 1916 Rising and the exact place where the Irish leaders were executed. Before we reached that gloomy courtyard draped in Irish green, orange and white patriotism, we wound our way through dark and dank stone hallways, which protected us from the bitter December winds. It felt like the inside of a cave and we shivered with cold. We stamped our numb toes and hugged our own frozen bodies while poking our heads into the damp cells and tried to visualize the plight of the prisoners. The numbing coldness wasn't hard to imagine; however, trying to envision some sixteen bodies stuffed into one small chamber with only a two-inch candle allotted each week, (to provide both light and warmth), was a more difficult undertaking.

Our guide told us that during the potato (pronounced pa-dáy-doe) famine of 1845-1850 when food was so scarce, homeless and destitute people often committed petty crimes just to have the shelter of the *gaol* and the scrap of bread doled out to prisoners each day.

A question arose regarding the potato famine and how a country bordered by sea could allow its people to starve. In a land with many large and navigable rivers with no part of the island more than fifty miles from tidewater, weren't fish plentiful and readily available to feed the masses?

We were told that Ireland was a nation of paupers and fish were a luxury that the ill-equipped fishermen couldn't acquire with their small boats. The herring fishermen were also too poor to buy salt to preserve their catch, and there was neither refrigeration nor railways to transport fish for sale to the masses.

The potato crop failed due to the late blight, the attacking disease also known as downy mildew and "rust." It was the only crop to fail during this period and according to a paper by Karis Wright, "wheat, oats, beef, mutton, pork and poultry were all in excellent supply but the Irish-English landlords shipped these to the European continent to soften the starving there and received a very good profit in return." Wright and others further suggest that due to the exclusive use of the potato as dietary mainstay of the rural people, English committees issued warnings that a failure of the crop would result in massive starvation. But the warnings were ignored and the Great Potato Famine resulted in a million and a half deaths and the emigration of another million to the United States and Canada.

My ancestors arrived in Boston during the Great Potato Famine. They were Catholic. My husbands' family is also of Catholic descent; however, as Americans became Episcopalians. This means little in Twenty-First Century America, but we find it curious that each of his three siblings married a Catholic. While I don't intend to explore the history of the religious disputes of the British Isles or the bitter struggle for Irish independence, I do think it's relevant to note that as American citizens, we were treated like royalty in Ireland.

As the memory of the Irish people is long, both their bitter struggles with England as well as their gratitude toward America for sending food during the famine are openly worn on their green sleeves. Every place we went, locals were happy to show us the way. From teaching us to order "crisps" instead of potato chips and "chips" instead of fries, to helping pick up my six-year-old daughter when she fell off her scooter, telling her she was "gorgeous in her little red coat," these happy people couldn't have been more accommodating.

On Christmas night we walked around old Dublin so my sister-in-law could point out a few more sites, including some of the infamous statues of Dublin: Molly Malone, known to locals as the "Tart with the Cart" and James Joyce, the "Dick with the Stick," to name two. As one of our companions sang "My Wild Irish Rose" at the top of his lungs, and spoke with a terrible Irish brogue, it wasn't difficult for passing strangers to guess we were American tourists. One young lass heard our conversation and stopped in her tracks saying, "Oh you're from America, are ya? Happy Christmas! And have you got anything to smoke?"

Many asked about September 11th and whether or not we knew anyone killed at the Pentagon or the World Trade Towers. They assured us that Ireland was behind us one hundred percent. God Bless America, they all said.

On the day after Christmas, a day known as St. Stephen's, we made like the locals and went to the races. We were assured it was the only thing to do as all the shops and restaurants remained closed. Our venue was Leopardstown and there we staked our ground in the concrete stands, a little island of Americans in the midst of a sea of Irish. The horse races were about twenty minutes apart, and as the crowds came and went, the afternoon had the web and flow of a tide. The stands were relatively bare between each race as most of the spectators ventured inside to the pubs to warm up with a pint of Guinness; however, we maintained our position due to the large size of our group (including lots of children) and our fear of getting separated. As the race start grew closer, the crowd filtered out and filled the stands around us. We all stood shoulder to shoulder with our children gripping our hands tightly or begging to be put up on our shoulders so they could see the sleek horses race past. We noticed how those immediately next to us hushed and leaned in a little to listen to our accents— the same way any of us might delight in hearing the musical sounds of an Irish accent while in the United States.

We still mimic the woman selling candy bars outside the gate ("three bars for a pound"), as we filed out with the masses, and at some point we learned while trying to meander through that sea of Guinness on legs that "excuse me," as a means of getting by doesn't work. "Sorry," you say instead, and the waters part. My sister-in-law already knew this, of course, but she let us discover some things about Ireland on our own.

I think back now to the days at my Catholic school and the green we proudly wore on St. Patrick's day and realize I didn't know the first thing about Irish pride. I'm grateful that my ancestors had the wherewithal to escape the potato famine and land on the shores of Massachusetts. But as a result of my visit to this beautiful green island, I can now wear green on St. Patrick's Day, say that I'm Irish and know what it really means.

I tip my hat to Professor Cozzens.

Kid Conversations

April 21, 1992

I had a phone conversation with my nephew the other day. It was an accident. He was keeping house while his mother was out fulfilling the chauffeur part of her chosen role in life (one of the younger boys had a birthday party to attend—or was it a soccer game?) and happened to pick up the phone when I called.

When you're the aunt to fifteen and have experienced a certain number of "kid conversations," this is not a situation you want to create for yourself too often—especially at long distance rates. One can endure only so many monosyllabic responses to mundane aunt questions like "How's school?"

Bryan, my oldest nephew, is fourteen. Since I've lived far away from him for most of these fourteen years, the telephone plays a major role in our relationship. He's well beyond the stage when the phone receiver acts only as a competition for his mother's attention. And our phone conversations are well beyond the stage of my sister asking: "Do you want to say hello to Bryan?"

"Hello B-B-B-B-B- Bryan ... "

Bryan's at an age when the art of conversation is just beginning to penetrate his lips. While the monosyllabic grunts are still very much a part of his manner, I have found that they only come in response to topics that don't interest him very much.

"Is your mom home?" I ask.

191

The Things I Wish I'd Said

"Nope."

"When's she coming back?"

"I dunno."

"Where'd she go?"

"Out."

Mom's responsibilities are obviously of little interest. So, I try again.

"Are you still playing basketball?"

"A little bit," says Bryan. "What's with the Golden State Warriors this year? How come they're doing so good?"

(I want desperately to correct his grammar—"how come they're doing so well?"—but I refrain. I'm too excited by the number of words put before me.)

Bryan's one of the millions of young fans who thinks that Michael Jordan and the Chicago Bulls are God's gift to the NBA—and to the world for that matter—so I realize this conversation will get into regional sports rivalries. Fine. We killed five minutes comparing the point guard capabilities between Tim Hardaway and John Paxson.

Through this juvenile banter I learn that he reads the sports pages. This makes me happy. He's reading, I think. Good sign. I use this as a transition to the most important aunt question:

"How's school?"

And this is when Bryan blows me away. Shame on me for expecting a mere grunt or the word "boring."

"It's great," he says with genuine enthusiasm. I can honestly say that I've never gotten this response from him or from anyone to whom I've ever posed this question.

"You're graduating this year—eighth grade, right?"

"Yeah. High school next year."

"Are you still all stressed out about your grades and getting into a good college?" I ask.

"Naw," says Bryan. "My grades are good. I'm lousy at math with algebra and all those stupid integers and stuff like that. But I'm good at, like, political science and government. I get the answers right on the tests and my friends ask, 'man, how do you get all those answers right,' and stuff."

Long distance minutes tallied up. My sister hadn't yet returned. "She'll be home any minute," he said. "You wanna hang on?"

I wasn't sure if he intended to continue the conversation or put me on hold. So, I opted to try and talk to his younger brother Brandon, who I heard banging around in the background. And this episode shoved me right back into my expectations of kid conversations.

"Hi Brandon," I say.

"Ugh," he grunts. (Translation: "Hi.")

"What are you doing?"

"Nuthin'."

"Is Easter still your favorite holiday?" I ask—proud that I remember how much he likes Easter.

"Naw," he moans. "I got these stupid cold sores all over the place . . ."

That was the last I heard from Brandon. Later my sister explained that Brandon's at the age—eleven—when his looks are just starting to be important. When he occasionally gets a cold sore or a zit, he doesn't want to leave the house. Who does?

I guess I have more in common with these kids than I realized.

Adult Conversations?

So, these kids are technically adults now and I haven't had a real conversation with Bryan since I kicked him out of my house for passing out in his mashed potatoes on Thanksgiving a few years back. And Brandon, who is now a pilot and working on a degree in aviation, speaks a language I hardly understand where everyone and everything is a "warts." He greets me by saying, "Yo, warts," or "Wassup, Auntie?" The last time he visited he slept until it was nearly dark and I accused him of being a vampire. I must have been busy feeding and bathing my little ones and getting them to bed so I could pass out in my own mashed potatoes, because I don't remember having much time to actually talk with him.

But if I had had a conversation, my questions wouldn't have evolved much beyond "how's school?" and "why do you wear your pants like that?"

The Things I Wish I'd Said

I'd like to think of myself as a cool aunt, but in their eyes I'll most likely always be an old fuddy-duddy. A fuddy-duddy with warts.

Descendents of Pocahontas

There's a book in the Montclair branch of the Oakland library called *The Double Life of Pocahontas*. I found it while looking for biographical information about the legendary Indian princess, Pocahontas.

Until recently, what I knew about Pocahontas was based only on what I could remember from a play we put on in Brownies, back when I was in third grade. I knew that she was a young Indian maiden who helped to bring peace between the Native Americans and the English settlers by her marriage to the gentleman John Rolfe. And I knew that my younger sister, Gayle, was chosen to act her role in the play because she was the prettiest (she was always the prettiest) and she had the longest hair, most feasible for braiding.

Today I know a bit more about Pocahontas, including the fact that if I should someday bear children, they will be her descendents.

As many families have a designated historian, my husband's aunt, Ellen, has spent a lot of time researching her family tree. Tracing the lines as far back as the early 1600s, she indeed discovered a direct tie to the only "famous" person on this list, Pocahontas.

Before this discovery, it may never have occurred to my pale-faced husband that he might have an ounce (or perhaps a drop) of Indian blood running through his veins. But he does. And to anyone interested in genealogy, his relation to Pocahontas has become a small source of pride.

• • •

The Things I Wish I'd Said

Over Labor Day weekend we went to Chicago to visit with my father-in-law in honor of his seventy-fifth birthday. Much of the time we were aboard his brand-new, sailing yacht, *Pocahontas* (which, by the way, means "playful one"). Not unlike my sister, *Pocahontas* was by far the prettiest boat in the harbor. Heads turned from every direction to look her over, admiring her size and newness. A colorful painting of the maiden's profile on the transom and a loose, artistic script proclaiming her name, gave her even more distinctiveness.

I was utterly enchanted with this sailboat even before we ventured out to the exhilarating, rough waters of Lake Michigan. Once the sails were up and we cut through the fresh, turquoise waves, I marveled at the quiet and the speed with which we raced past the expansive Chicago skyline. The serenity was enough to make me swear off motorboats forever.

Later that evening, we left *Pocahontas* behind and walked across the street from the harbor to Grant Park and milled about the field of people who were there for the annual Chicago Jazz Festival.

The music was moody. One minute it made me want to dance. The next minute the sounds were so sultry that I felt intoxicated. With the serene, mysterious waters to the east and the powerful, noisy city streets to the west, I felt a little off balance, unable to adjust my new-found sea legs to the ground below.

I leaned against the fence in front of me, soaking in the warm, breezy night, and suddenly it hit me like a three-foot wave: My God, I thought, Chicago is a beautiful, beautiful place. Why didn't I realize this while living there? Why was I so anxious to leave my Midwestern roots, my home, and travel so far away to live in California?

Like Pocahontas, I guess, who changed her name to Rebecca and traveled to England with her husband, I too, committed to a life in California to be with the man to whom I am married.

I've been in California for many years now. I call this place my home. But I have to admit that there is an enormous part of me yearning for whatever it is about the Midwest that keeps pulling me back again and again and makes me cry when it is time to leave.

The Double Life of Pocahontas indicated that "Rebecca" wanted to stay in England where she was received as a princess. Yet there was another book on the library shelf, *Pocahontas and the Strangers*, which suggested the opposite. In this story, Pocahontas was anxious to leave England and return to Virginia.

Regardless, she never made it back because at the age of twenty-two, she died of small pox.

One thing both books reported was that Pocahontas was not fond of sailing on the rough, gray waters of the Atlantic.

I wonder how she would have felt about Lake Michigan.

Raising Princesses

My two daughters, direct descendants of Pocahontas, understand that they are her kin, but I don't think either realizes it has nothing to do with Walt Disney. They see the Indian Princess not as a human being, but as a celluloid character with Barbie Doll proportions, big, Disney leading lady eyes and a spectacular singing voice.

I don't know where the *Pocahontas* is today, but I imagine she's somewhere in Europe, where she was sold several years ago. My father-in-law, who by the way loved the above column and gave me a Madame Alexander's Pocahontas doll as a Christmas present that year, sold his trophy sailing vessel shortly after we turned down an offer to use her for a charter sailing business.

Since we loved to sail, my husband and I actually considered accepting the yacht and creating a rather Bohemian lifestyle for ourselves in the Bahamas or the Florida Keys. We went as far as to enroll in sailing lessons that would have led to obtaining skipper's licenses had we not quit.

Ultimately we did return to the Midwest and decided against spending the rest of our lives at sea. We both knew we wanted to have children one day and believed that the future descendants of Pocahontas should be raised on land. Not on a *Pocahontas*.

Chapter 5
Aging, Death, Grief

Cowards die many times before their deaths;

The valiant never taste of death but once.

Of all the wonders that I yet have heard,

It seems to me most strange that men should fear;

Seeing that death, a necessary end,

Will come when it will come.

—William Shakespeare, *Julius Caesar*

Big Beautiful Mama of Bali

Picture this. You're driving your car, speeding probably, and suddenly you find yourself stuck behind a slow moving vehicle. Seeing only a shock of white hair and hands at the ten and two o'clock positions gripped tightly on the steering wheel of some 1960s American model car, you curse this elderly driver—this road block—who is keeping you from hurrying to your destination.

It happens all the time.

We have a vision of the elderly that usually brings to mind words like feeble and worn, names like grandma and grandpa. We see gray hair and wrinkles, canes and wheelchairs.

We don't like to think about it, really. But sometimes we must. Because even though we fend it off as much as possible, we are all aging. And if we're lucky enough to have long, healthy lives, we know that someday it just might be us behind the wheel with an aggravated driver beeping the horn.

I met someone the other day who taught me a great deal about what it means to age. Her name is Dr. Marilyn Ducati. She is a sixty year-old gerontologist who is about to embark upon an adventure around the world. And she's doing it alone.

Before meeting Dr. Ducati face-to-face, I spoke to her on the phone several times. Since she told me almost immediately that she was sixty years old I had to struggle to picture the face behind such a lively, youthful voice.

The Things I Wish I'd Said

Laced with a few telltale New York corners, her accent indicated she was not a native of the Bay Area. But soon I learned that she has worked in Oakland for fifteen years and owns a home in Piedmont, which she has rented in order to provide a small income to support her upcoming travels.

Ducati, tall, blonde and beautiful, has spent most of her career working with the elderly and says she has heard the words, "If only I . . ." many, many times. "As people told me of the missed opportunities in their life-times, it taught me that there is a severe penalty for procrastination," she said. "So I want to travel while I still can."

The mother of three grown daughters, Ducati says they think she's a little crazy for planning to traipse off to such exotic ports as Fiji, Bali, Auckland, parts of Thailand and India, (and if finances permit, she'd like to make it to Africa); however, she feels her quest is very important.

"Travelers have a certain spirit," she said. "We're people who want to know where in the world is the best place for me. And if you're free, like I am, and are able to conquer your fears, it's amazing what you can do."

An award winning poet, the author of Reflections: *The Joy of Life*, a book of poetry, and a book on the elderly, *Before My Time*, Ducati is planning to write a book about her upcoming travels, called *Around the World at 60*.

"The purpose of this book is to encourage older people who don't have a lot of money and who aren't in the best of health to get out there and see the world if that's what they have always wanted to do," she said. "You have to have courage and ask yourself, if not now, when?"

Probably the strongest message Ducati conveys is that age doesn't have to be a factor when it comes to fulfilling your dreams.

"I even joined a youth hostel to get a card," she said. "Youth has nothing to do with the acceptance of people around the world. You just have to be outgoing and friendly enough to reach out and embrace people," she said. "They will show you places you would have never found otherwise."

She recalled a former trip to Bali where she spent two months relaxing in the healing tropical waters and walking down Monkey Forest Road, meeting new friends daily. While there, she met a special old man, a friend she called Papa, who gave her the endearing nickname, Big Beautiful Mama.

After spending a morning with her in her friend's apartment in Oakland, where she is staying these last two weeks before her trip, it was easy for me to see that Dr. Ducati indeed makes friends easily.

I look forward to hearing of her travels and sharing them with you.

If You Have To Ask

Marilyn Ducati was a Mensa member. Since I had to ask her what that meant, I might just as easily stuck my finger on my chin and burped the word, "duh."

Mensa, an organization founded in England in 1946, is for individuals who have an extraordinarily high IQ. They test in the top two percent in the nation. There are roughly 100,000 Mensa members worldwide and half of them are in the United States, which means there's room for about 5.5 million more in the land of the free and the home of the brains. (I did a quick math problem to figure out two percent of our current population, which no doubt makes me a genius if I'm correct or a dope if I'm wrong.) We've got some famous Mensans in these United States including the actress Geena Davis, the author Jean Auel, the master of the pun, Richard Lederer and, of course, the queen of the Mensans, Marilyn Vos Savant, who is listed in the *Guinness Book of World Records* for having the highest IQ on record, which is something like two-thousand.

Clearly, I'm not a member and it was only recently—when I deviated from my online Enneagram research and took an IQ test—that I discovered I have a respectable IQ. The results called me both a "facts curator" and a "word warrior," and even used the term "brainiac."

Whew!

Whether or not my score on that particular, unsupervised test qualifies me for Mensa membership is unknown and unimportant, primarily because these days I live by a motto centered on the words, "where good enough is." And I think my IQ is simply good enough.

Besides, I think IQ tests are more about testing one's ability to do IQ tests and less about actually measuring one's intelligence quotient.

• • •

The Things I Wish I'd Said

After the above column ran in the paper, I received a brief note of thanks from the big, beautiful mama of Bali and then never heard from her again. I found a copy of her book, *Before My Time*, at a used bookstore and thought it a was funny, well-written story about an old woman named Fanny Bloom and her dismay over being placed in a nursing home; however, the typeface used to publish it was the pica cursive ball on an IBM Selectric typewriter, which made it difficult to read. I could easily read that kind of type when it was in style like platform shoes and Farrah Fawcett hair in the 1970s and even the early 1980s, but after that, my type needed serifs and kerning. (If you have to ask what serifs or kerning are, you are not a typeface connoisseur on *my* level. I test high in the area of typeface knowledge due to years working in graphic design and typography studios and am fairly sure I rank in the top two percent of the nation.) To my knowledge the book Marilyn Ducati foresaw about her travels around the world was never published. Perhaps she's still writing it while hanging out in some youth hostel in Southeast Asia. I'll keep checking Amazon.com, the card catalogue at my fingertips. Meanwhile, I hope she's traded in her typewriter for a laptop, and I hope she continues to set the world straight on the value of the elderly.

Meanwhile, the concept of aging hit me smack in the face this evening when my daughter Willow asked me to help with the part of her homework requiring adult participation. She brings home 8-1/2 x 11-inch homework packets each week and the opening pages always have assignments to include your "grownup." Your grownup, inevitably me, participates by answering questions or playing a game, which I inevitably lose. (I'm quite sure my gifted and talented Mensa-bound daughter studies the problems in advance and sets me up for loss after humiliating loss.) Tonight's assignment: Aging. The homework packet, without any regard for manners, asked for "your grownup's" age, and even asked her to double-check my response by requiring the year of my birth in question two. Of course, Willow knew the answers without asking and filled in the blanks while I supervised.

This was actually an easy homework participation assignment for me—a good thing since I was getting ready to go to a candle party, which is a twenty-first century version of a Tupperware party made of wax instead of plastic, and requires only a double-digit IQ. Anyway, as she rattled off the questions, each question made me ten years older. "How old will your grownup be in ten years? And in twenty years?" And so on, until I had outlived the Russian yogurt-eaters we used to see advertising Dannon on TV. I grew so old just standing in my kitchen that I was about to order a wheelchair to get to the candle party next door.

My life is going fast enough that I don't need to project to ages that will make me officially old. I'm already wearing reading glasses and driving slower (especially at night) and have to endure flashing headlights in my rearview mirror from "youngsters" in a great big damn hurry. They roar past me in their throbbing pick-up trucks where the bass on their electronic sound machines is turned up so high that even through my closed windows it sounds like a heartbeat on a fetal monitor. In our relatively rural corner of the desert we don't have many passing lanes, but we do have stoplights. And inevitably these same kids end up idling next to me, revving up the gas peddle like it's a musical instrument, poised to push it to the floor the second the light blinks from red to green.

My own kids think I'm old as dust and my soccer team just thinks I'm something to jump on each time we get in a huddle and I ask them to "take a knee." The teenagers in the Sunday school class think of me as an old person trying hard to act cool to keep their attention. And then there are my nephews. To them I'm old *and* boring.

Last week I visited with my nephews (one is driving, the other is old enough to drink) and they seemed particularly grown up as they sat next to us at the "adult's table." As we passed jokes back-and-forth, my husband suggested I tell these boys a dirty joke I keep in my back pocket, which in the right circles guarantees a laugh. I didn't think they were ready for this particular joke; however, my husband assured me with a Monty Python nudge and wink that they'd "get it."

I had their full attention through most of the joke as they nodded and smiled conspiratorially. "I'm giving my boyfriend the nickname Mountain Dew. Because he likes to mount me and he always do." But then came the punch line about Grand Mariner being a "fine liquor."

The Things I Wish I'd Said

"Mmm-mmmm," I said, as I've said fifty times before. And they both stared at me with what looked like my husband's face twenty years ago. Their blank expressions clearly said, "what-is she-talking-about?"

"You don't get it, do you," I said.

"No," they uttered in unison and turned away to talk about *Star Wars* or Hip Hop or some such topic beyond my scope. I elbowed my husband (hard) and said I *knew* they weren't ready for that joke. (Clearly, neither had ever gone down on a woman because if they had, they would have realized that I actually said "licker," instead of liquor, and they would have laughed.)

Blame it on the age difference. Or better yet, blame it on virginity.

My nephews not getting this joke didn't make me boring and didn't make them thick. On the contrary, these are extraordinarily bright young men and I, of course, am certainly not boring! It just goes to show you, anyone can take an IQ test and claim they're a brainiac; however, nothing beats experience.

And nothing beats the pleasure of a fine liquor. Mmm-*mmmm*.

Woman's Best Friend

May 7, 1991

She was born with eight siblings in a trailer park in southern Illinois. The runt of the litter, for the first six weeks of her life she was her owners' favorite. But soon she was given to me.

"What's with the eyes?" I asked upon seeing my puppy for the first time. They were huge—like prize aggies—one gleaming auburn-brown, the other as blue as a swimming pool.

"Her mom's a husky," replied the owner. "Her father is the big, black lab who lives on the other side of the park. He's up for Father-of-the-Year around here."

I adopted this adorable puppy, daughter of a blue-eyed beauty and the Don Juan of the trailer park, almost eleven years ago. I named her Shonah. It's a pretty name; that's why I chose it. But whenever I meet a woman named Shonah, rather than blurt out, "Ha! That's my dog's name;" I usually twist the truth and say that Shonah (pronounced Sha´-na) had been named after the Shawnee National Forest, which surrounded the area where she was born.

Like me, Shonah has been a California girl for nine years. That's most of her life not mine. Although she never had puppies (as I exercised our right to choose and had her spade at six months of age), I believe she has had a full, happy life.

She knows all the crowd-pleasers like, "Sit, shake, lie down, and roll over." And she knows the master-pleasers like "stay" and "come here, now!" Shonah will fetch the stick or Frisbee, but she won't bring it back. And keep her away from farms with chicken coops because there won't be any eggs for breakfast the next day—bird dog that she is.

There have been plenty of times when she has been naughty and even obstinate by deliberately taking off to explore the neighborhood (usually in the middle of a bath). But undeniably, she has been a wonderful pet. Woman's best friend.

And now I'm facing for the first time what every pet owner must eventually endure. My little girl, Shonah, is dying.

It came on suddenly. One morning she was simply hobbling. At first I thought she had pulled a muscle during her afternoon run or while jumping out the back of the truck. But even after three weeks of prescribed rest, the hobble would not go away. Then the whimpering started and it soon turned to outright crying. I felt as helpless as a new mother with a whaling baby in her arms.

The word from Vet Number One was arthritis, prescription aspirin. That wasn't enough. Vet Number Two was more thorough, however, and $375 later, we had arthritis complicated by a light neurological disorder with the possibility of tumors inflicting pain around her neck and shoulders.

Lord, help us.

For a week I've been lacing her morning and evening chow with all kinds of drugs. And since the whimpering has subsided, she seems to be getting better with this first step of the treatment. To say the least, I'm relieved.

My main concern has been her pain. Secondly, however, I am concerned about her quality of life. She has been a very active dog, used to popping up as soon as she sees anybody change into action shoes. The vet says she shouldn't be walked for more than one block per day—if that.

We have another dog, Stella, who is also pushing age eleven (that's seventy-seven to you and me). Except for a lack of front teeth and weakening hind legs, she's still spry and raring to go. When Shonah sees us leave for an afternoon of running, squirrel chasing and rolling in whatever dead thing we can find, those sad, exotic eyes of hers' nearly break my heart.

She knows she's being left behind. But I assure her that we'll be home soon.

Unconditional Love

This column generated a huge response. I received both empathy and sympathy calls and in one case, a call from someone insisting my dog had Lymes Disease and I should treat her accordingly. She didn't have this disease, but I was grateful for the outpouring of concern over my pet.

The first thing journalism students are taught in their early news writing courses is the catchy adage, "When dog bites man it isn't news. But when man bites dog, it's news." Obviously this is meant to be a figurative lesson. But I think when it comes to our dogs; we perk up our ears to hear any story about our canine companions and chew on the details like a juicy steak bone. Every week there's a dog story on the news or in the paper.

A while back I learned a dog was spotted running around the deck of an abandoned Indonesian tanker adrift off the coast of the Hawaiian Islands. Apparently a fire crippled the ship and when the crew was rescued nearly three weeks later, the poor dog was forgotten. He was spotted from the air pacing the decks, perhaps signaling the helicopter with a doggy SOS. Upon the sighting report, the Hawaiian Humane Society sprung to action and a $50,000 air-and-sea rescue campaign ensued. The funds were used up after five days of trying to relocate the burned-out vessel without luck. So, with $25,000 from a $50 million fund from the federal Oil Pollution Act of 1990, the Coast Guard took over the task of locating the vessel and rescuing the castaway dog, a two-year-old terrier named Forgea. She belonged to the captain, who didn't go down with the ship. From the original crew consisting of a captain and ten men, only the dog, the body of one crewman, and more than 60,000 gallons of fuel remained aboard. And while I believe the Coast Guard's main concern was the tanker running aground and polluting the sensitive marine environment near Johnson Island, a former chemical weapons disposal facility turned wildlife preserve, what made this a newsworthy story was the castaway dog—a canine in Tom Hanks clothing.

Shortly after the Forgea story, in Tucson, a puppy was found skinned alive. The dog was in so much pain it had to be euthanized and a $20,000 award for the capture of the perpetrator soon arose. Cruelty to animals of this magnitude, we learned, is a key trait exhibited by budding serial killers or child molesters.

We learn a lot through our dogs.

Shonah was my first dog—or I should say the first dog I got to keep for over a week. Since the day I was fourteen and rescued an abandoned puppy from the sticks of Missouri, whom I named "Star" and loved wholeheartedly for three days before my father took him to the Humane Society with a ten-dollar donation, I wanted a dog in my life. My parents didn't allow them for reasons swirling around "allergies" and my mom's full plate. Most people know puppies may make great Christmas presents, but kids have short attention spans. When they lose interest, feeding, walking and brushing the dog ends up as another job for Mom. (My mom housebroke five kids. She didn't need a dog.) But apparently, I felt I needed a dog.

Through Shonah I learned about unconditional love. It didn't take long to notice that she was always happy to see me. I also learned a thing or two about the cost of veterinarians and keeping her healthy on a college student's wages. On the day Ronald Reagan was elected to the White House she had an unpleasant encounter with a speeding car, and I started a payment plan for her surgery that lasted through a good part of his administration. I learned about the difficulties of finding a rental unit allowing dogs and then learned about living with fleas and fighting the battle to keep them at bay.

I learned about neglect and how easy it was to ignore her. She developed a habit of running off whenever it was time to leave the house and I grew enraged each time I had to strike out with a search party to find her. I took it personally, like she purposefully wanted to upset me, or worse, get away from me. Yet even after days of selfishness on my behalf, she never failed to greet me with a wagging tail and a canine smile.

In the end, we grew as close as a woman and her pet could be. And when I faced her dying eyes, I was shocked at how hard it hit me. Prior to my experience with Shonah, I had only heard about the amount of work involved in taking care of a dog and the joy one reaps through this companionship. No one told me about the part when they die.

Now I know how that feels.

Playing God and Losing

August 13, 1991

There's a small wooden box on a shelf in our living room. Although it's nicely handcrafted, even pretty, it's as nondescript as a wooden box can be. It could contain jewelry, matches, even Tarot cards wrapped in a silk scarf.

But it doesn't.

The box is locked. A miniature gold-colored padlock, probably easily picked with a nail file, keeps its contents safe from accidental exposure. Curious as anyone might be, I don't think the remains of my dog, Shonah, would be very pleasant to the eye. Because that's what's inside this box, this coffin, this urn. I don't really know what to call it. And even worse, I don't know what to do with it.

Shonah would have been eleven years old on the first of August. But she was stricken with a crippling illness and diagnosed with cancer last May. Her demise was so sudden that she seemingly went from puppy to senior in the blink of her brown and blue eyes.

I'd like to take this opportunity to thank Drs. Eric Braun and Lauren Knobel at Skyline Veterinary Hospital for guiding Shonah and me through the end of her life. Although each time I left their office and drove teary-eyed on those hairpin turns along Skyline Boulevard back toward my house, they helped me to believe that everything was going to be all right.

When I was called upon to take a turn at "playing God" and pulled the word "euthanasia" intimately into my vocabulary, they, in a quiet, confident

213

manner assured me that I was doing the right thing. Shonah was probably in a lot of pain, they said.

The decision to euthanize Shonah was mine alone to make. I found it interesting that these veterinarians as well as the neurologist they sent us to in order to confirm their suspicions of a tumor never mentioned the word "euthanasia" until it came from me.

I had only associated mercy killing with "moral decision" classes and heated debates with Karen Ann Quinlan as a case study. More recently I've read about AIDS patients and their loved ones fighting the issue in courtrooms across the country. And recently on *The Today Show*, I saw a member of The Hemlock Society promoting his book about how to die with dignity. An opposing viewpoint claimed he was pushing suicide.

As far as pets are concerned, I heard about them being "put to sleep" routinely and for as long as I can remember. It was no big deal. But when it was my turn to confront this issue, I was a mess. As I mused out loud, "What am I going to do?" The doctors met my eyes with strong, concerned looks. "Do I put her to sleep?" I asked.

I was told that given the diagnosis, euthanasia wouldn't be the wrong thing to do. Then all the details: Do you want to be present? What do you want to do with her remains? Would you like information on a pet loss support group? Going into mechanical mode, I answered these questions.

I cried yesterday. Today I must be strong.

Losing Shonah was my first real experience with death. It took me a month to stop looking for her when I came home. And even now I have to work through my memories to recall her as a puppy and a young, active, healthy dog. I keep picturing her as this sad black lump resting, dying in her favorite spot on the side of the house.

I think of all those times I took her existence for granted. And I miss her so much. More than I thought possible.

It has been suggested that we get another puppy, and believe me, each week when this newspaper runs photos of dogs to adopt, I study it like a catalog. But like shopping without money, it's like adoption without ambition. I'm afraid I'd be trying to replace Shonah. And I don't think it should be that way.

For now I still have her with me—if that's what's really inside the small wooden box that I know I'll never open. I had envisioned scattering her ashes at Berkeley's Aquatic Park, her favorite disc golf course, but that was before the box arrived from the crematorium.

I guess all questions cannot be answered right away and decisions will be made in time.

Playing God is really tough.

Death on Sugar Mountain

I read this column and missed my dog all over again. But that doesn't surprise me. It's my naiveté that I find perplexing. This was "my first real experience with death," I wrote.

I used the word "first," yet I meant, and wished I'd said, "only." The use of the word "first" seemed to indicate I was aware there'd be a second, third and fourth experience with death. Maybe I thought losing my dog might prepare me for the death to come.

It didn't.

A dozen years later, and after suffering a series of deaths in my family, I have a view of death so affected it has left me looking into the mirror at a strange, aged face. I've reached a point where I've learned that age isn't just a number or a date on your driver's license. It's a condition of life, like terms on a contract to which one never really agrees. Aging is a condition, I believe, that the longer it prevails, the more it puts you face-to-face with death.

Shortly after saying goodbye to Shonah, my aunt died. A few years later we lost my father-in-law. The next summer it was my mother's turn to go and six months after that, another aunt. The following month my mother-in-law died, followed by an uncle and then another aunt. The World War II generation on my husband's side of the family has disappeared from the face of the earth. And while my octogenarian father and his older brothers are alive and well, I now know that if all goes according to "plan," we will face more funerals in the future.

But life doesn't always go according to plan. Just when we thought we had once again lapsed into a routine lull, we faced a sudden and dramatic dip—a brutal reminder of the roller coaster ride tracking together our years.

It was February, 2002 and we had spent the weekend in Scottsdale, Arizona visiting my brother-in-law, in town on business. After making the two-hour drive home to Tucson, we progressed into school-night mode and settled in for the evening. The kids were fed and bathed, stories were about to be read and good night kisses administered. Then the phone rang.

It wasn't an ominous death ring like the ring in the middle of the night when we learned my father-in-law had died. It was just a normal, early evening ring and my husband answered.

"Is Aunt Michele there?" asked the caller.

"Who wants to know?" teased my husband, aware it was our teenaged nephew.

"Is Aunt Michele there?" he asked again, and with a blank expression, my husband handed me the phone.

"Hello?"

"Aunt Michele?"

"Yes?"

"Stephanie had . . . Stephanie, uh, had, uh, a heart attack."

I sat up straight and instinctively grabbed my own heart. "What did you say?"

Momentarily, there was an awful silence. A buzz filled my eager ear. "Here," said my nephew, and I heard the phone exchange hands.

"She collapsed at work," said my brother. "I don't know what they're telling me," he managed in a tone I didn't recognize. My big brother's voice, a voice, which was usually deep and monotonous, was now minute and pained, like a pinprick or a tinkle—a small bell instead of a gong. He said they were at the hospital.

"We'll be right there," I said, pushing the off button on the phone. I dropped it on my bed onto an open newspaper, and at once the air in the room became terrible and suffocating. "We have to go," I said to my husband. "Stephanie had a heart attack."

When I said the words "heart attack" out loud, it somehow made this unfathomable news true. But I still didn't want to believe it. Fighting with reality on our fifteen-minute drive to the hospital, I began a horrible diatribe with God. It might have qualified as prayer, but it felt more like desperate, pathetic pleading. I begged for this so-called heart attack to be untrue—to be a minor, insignificant event. I argued with its possibility. "Not Stephanie," I cried. "She's only twenty! Please God, make this not be happening. Make it all a terrible mistake." I couldn't stop hitting the dashboard of our car and by the time we parked, I was on the edge of hysteria.

While life's roller coaster sped downward at a perverse angle, we sprinted to the hospital waiting room and met the pale and confused faces of our family. And there, we took up residence for the next two days.

Stephanie Rose, a statuesque, redheaded beauty, was a girl my mom called "stop-traffic gorgeous." She had a brief modeling career in high school and then chose work over college after her graduation. She had only lived in Tucson for three months. In November, 2001, along with her family, she moved from the concrete cornfields of Naperville, Illinois to the cactus-covered land of the Sonoran desert when her dad transferred jobs.

On February 6 we celebrated her twentieth birthday and under our poolside *ramada* I sang Neil Young's "Sugar Mountain" to her while she rolled her eyes at me for the thousandth time. *"You can't be twenty on Sugar Mountain. Though you think you're leaving there too soon."* It turns out she had already known this. After an extended excursion in the mountains of southern Colorado where she went after high school and then another year at home with her parents, her stint on Sugar Mountain *was* over and planned to attend Arizona State University the following fall semester.

But she never made it. Two weeks after her twentieth birthday, she died.

Stephanie was born with a congenital heart defect that made her cyanotic as a child. The situation was corrected by a series of surgeries, the first at birth, the last at age thirteen. With the exception of a cool blue hue to her skin before the final surgery, by the size of her no one would guess she had a heart condition. Most babies with this defect, which continually robs the blood of oxygen, are frail, and she was expected to be sleepy and listless. But this was never the case with our tall and striking Stephanie. She came through each procedure bigger and stronger while her parents, as stoic as parents can be while their child undergoes a series of open-heart surgeries, became experts on the subject of her heart malformation. In her lifetime, they spent far too much time in doctor's offices, hospital waiting rooms and Ronald McDonald Houses and each time their child's chest was cracked open and the worst could happen, it never did. The miracles of modern medicine were on their side. Since her final surgery, Stephanie had had a clean bill of health. For all practical purposes, we believed she was a normal girl.

But Stephanie was not normal. And her heart had anything but a normal reaction to the dietary supplement she took, which caused her heart to stop.

It was Stephanie's first night waiting tables on the northeast side of town at a small, family restaurant. By day she worked the lunch shift on Tucson's "restaurant row," but took on a second job to save money for college. She had been on the job for two hours when she collapsed. And whether or not the diners thought it was anything more than a clumsy move behind the cubicle walls of the waitress station is unknown. But those witnessing the crash saw that the new girl, the tall one with the thick red curls, had collapsed.

An off-duty paramedic, a diner at the restaurant, sprung into action. He assessed her and administered CPR. Someone called 9-1-1 and an ambulance arrived. The paddles came out. They shocked her on the scene but it was two hours before a normal heart rhythm was reestablished. Two hours. Today I know what that means. A brain deprived of oxygen for more than twenty minutes (even with multiple shockings and CPR) is a brain that can shut down bodily functions one at a time.

Once the heart rhythm was established, she was on full support—a ventilator hose in her mouth, a network of IV tubes jabbed into her arms. "If recovery is going to happen, it's going to happen in the next forty-eight hours," said the doctors. "You can be hopeful because she is young. She has this on her side."

And then there was a statement we didn't expect.

"We just got the results of the tox-screen and Stephanie tested positive for amphetamines," said the emergency room physician. "What was she taking?"

"Amphetamines?" we gasped. "What do you mean amphetamines?" My mind flipped like a Rolodex, racing through a list of everything it knew to be an amphetamine. Cocaine? Street speed? Good Lord, Crystal Meth?

"No chance," I said, believing my niece was very straight-laced. "Not this kid."

"The test is positive," he said. "You should look through her purse to try and find the substance."

The only substance Stephanie's mother found was a dietary supplement with a label reading "All Natural," which certainly made it appear both legal and safe. Stephanie had purchased it on the Internet to help her shed a few pounds. Could it have contained something to make her test positive for amphetamines?

After the kidney specialist examined her, he said there was no reason a girl her age should have experienced a heart attack. When we mentioned that she was born with a heart defect he said it shouldn't have mattered. "It was corrected by her surgeries," he said. Stephanie's mother suggested that perhaps the heart attack was caused by whatever made her test positive for amphetamines. And without another word, the doctor turned and walked toward her room—a room in the critical care ward that by this point was guarded by a spawn of Nurse Rachett, who kept a close watch on the comings and goings of all of her patient's relatives. It was where the dietary supplement had been stored. Two minutes later he stomped back toward our huddle. He held the container in the air and shook it like a maraca.

"Worst possible thing," he said. "Worst possible thing she could have taken." (Our faces were as blank as any faces reacting to information difficult to understand.) *Ma Huang,*" he said loudly. "Ephedra—*Ma Huang*—is a Chinese herb. It made her test positive for amphetamines. Other people might be able to take this but for her? Worst possible thing." Then he shook his head in disgust and walked away. We never saw him again.

The news hit us like a kick in the gut. We suddenly knew this wasn't about her heart being a time bomb—we knew it was a terrible, terrible accident. Had she (or any of us) known of the dangers of this herb, this thing called ephedra, this nightmare could have been avoided.

After that, all we had left to do was wait. And pray. The scale weighing hope and despair hung in the room like a tangible piece of bric-a-brac. Despair = two hours without a heart rhythm. Hope = age twenty.

We couldn't talk about the ephedra. No one wanted to upset the balance.

After the first twenty-four hours of her coma, Stephanie no longer breathed ahead of the respirator or produced any urine, meaning her lungs and kidneys had shut down. Hours later a CAT scan showed swelling, edema, on the brain. Doctors started using terms like "vegetative state" and asked about signing a "DNR" just in case her heart stopped again.

It was just before the last grains of sand in that forty-eight hour glass hit the bottom of the despair side of the scale, that Stephanie's parents were forced to make the most difficult decision of their lives. They turned off the respirator and said goodbye to their child.

I think back to the day I said goodbye to my dog and the genuine sorrow that welled up inside me, yet it was nothing compared to the insurmountable grief caused by my niece's death. And I realize I made a mistake by writing that I played the role of God in choosing for my dog to be put to sleep.

If God has a game plan, the only rule I can think of is that we are not entitled to "play" Him. If we try, we'll fail.

So, I ask, was Stephanie's death a failure? And if the answer is yes, to whom do we attribute this failure? The doctors? No. They did all they could. Her parents? Certainly not. They provided her with the best possible medical care since the day of her birth. I know in their pain and sadness, which comes in waves of nausea at any time for understandable reasons and for no reason at all, they want to blame themselves for not monitoring the vitamins and dietary supplements their usually highly cautious daughter took. But she was twenty. She owned a credit card and had access to the Internet. She may have lived under their roof at the time, but she made adult decisions every day. We train our children to do this and by age twenty, most of them are well on their way to making their own decisions about nearly everything.

Which brings us to Stephanie herself. Do we blame her? Maybe. Yes, because she's the one who ingested the substance that stopped her heart. She's the one who felt she wasn't as skinny as the airbrushed, anorexic, boob-job babes in *Victoria's Secret* catalogs, and wanted to shed the pounds she had gained since her days as a high school model. And yet no, because she took a readily available substance and thought it contained non-threatening ingredients. She equated the words "all natural" on the bottle with the word "safe." And she made a deadly mistake.

After Stephanie's death our family took on the cause of educating the public on the potential dangers of unregulated herbs, particularly targeting the herb "ephedra." We called our grassroots organization, "HerBeware," raised money and spread literature. But it wasn't until February, 2003, a year after we lost her, when professional baseball player Steve Bechler of the Baltimore Orioles died of heat stroke during Spring training and the autopsy showed traces of ephedra in his system, that suddenly ephedra became front-page news. Already banned in the military, college sports, the NFL and the country of Canada, it would be another year before the FDA—the organization that truly holds the power of God—finally took measures to ban this potentially deadly herb.

Stephanie is gone and her immediate family will never be the same. The pain won't go away. But at the very least, the dangers of ephedra are now well publicized, and knowing that other families may be able to avoid this terrible fate does provide some comfort.

In my twenties, life was about weddings. In my thirties it was about baby showers. In my forties, it's about funerals. And while the wedding and shower phases will most likely repeat themselves in a generational way, I'm afraid the funerals are here to stay. The longer we live, the more death we experience. But has the experience of tucking this life lesson into the notebook of my mind made losing a loved one any easier?

Hell no.

Summer of Old

Date?

It was a summer day in a suburban backyard. Sitting in lawn chairs on a cement patio were neighborhood mothers drinking coffee and talking mother talk. Their young children kept the swing set squeaking in the distance, their shouts and giggles blending with the buzzing drone of Midwestern cicada.

Two young girls, one eleven, the other twelve, competed to see who could swing the highest. Their skinny legs worked hard as they pumped their way into the sky, and with each arc the metal legs of the swing set lifted off the ground like a rocking chair. When the girls finally reached their limits, they let go of the chains and plunged into the soft green grass.

It was a draw.

"I bet my mother is smarter than your mother," said the twelve-year-old suddenly.

"No way," said the other girl. "My mother is older than yours. Everybody knows that older means wiser."

"Naugh aw," the twelve-year-old cried. "My mother got out of school last and that means she remembers more stuff they taught her. Your mom is so much older than my mom that she's probably forgotten everything by now."

This sort of made sense to the eleven-year-old, but she wouldn't give in. "I think my mother's smarter than your mother," she said.

"Okay then," said the twelve-year-old, "we'll prove my mother's smarter by giving them a test. We'll ask them both how many miles it is to go from here to Philadelphia."

The eleven-year-old, thinking this sounded like a fair test, agreed.

Leaving the pendulating swings behind, the two girls marched toward the patio where their mothers sat next to each other cross-legged. Wasting no time in proving her mother was the smarter; the eleven-year-old quickly asked her how many miles it was to Philadelphia.

"I don't know," said her mother, who sipped her coffee and failed to see the look of disappointment on her daughter's face.

"My mother knows," bragged the twelve-year-old. "Right Mom?"

"Well, I think it's about 750 miles," she said. "We're planning a trip there next month for my cousin's wedding."

"See!" shouted the twelve-year-old. "I told you so."

The eleven-year-old, not realizing that the test was rigged, walked back toward the swing set feeling ashamed because her mother had failed her.

Her mother was fifty-three. At the time, the eleven-year-old-girl figured that was more than half of 100 and that was too old. She had never even known her grandparents and figured that if she were to have children some day, they probably wouldn't know their grandparents either.

She felt gypped.

Thirty years ago it was rare for women to bare children past the age of forty. (One exception: My Catholic family. Numbers five and six were conceived by "accident," and I was one of them.) More commonly, women bore their children early and certainly lived to see their grandchildren.

We've all seen this trend change in recent years as women have become more career-oriented and now tend to wait longer to start their families. The eleven-year-old with the over-fifty mom is no longer considered unusual.

Today, however, I'm a thirty-one year-old with a seventy-three year-old mother. That's not too common. I feel like I only recently got to an age where I could relate to her and my dad as people rather than Mommy and Daddy and now I'm watching them age.

It seems to have happened over night. Suddenly I find myself calling them "Pop-pop and Na-na" just like their nine grandchildren. And I also find myself tuning out while this white-haired man recalls yet another World War II story and this small, wrinkled lady tells me about an upcoming trip to South Carolina for the third time that evening.

"How many miles away is that?" I want to ask.

I feel, suddenly, like grains of salt falling in a three-minute egg timer are measuring my time with my parents. And I feel guilty because I think of things I'd rather be doing instead. I feel angry because they're getting old and there's nothing I can do about it.

I feel like that eleven-year-old girl walking toward a swing set wanting only to fly off into the sky.

I feel gypped.

Summer of the Redbird

I didn't include that my mother's favorite word was "shit." But I wish I had. She had never used or even heard the word until she was married and had her first job. One of her coworkers said it and my mom "liked the way it sounded." She especially liked the way it sounded in multiples. "Shit, shit, shit," is what I usually heard when she was mad or frustrated.

Now I'm a forty-something year-old girl and my mother is dead. She's been dead for five years and that pang of feeling ripped off continually creeps up on me without warning. I am a motherless child. At any age, that's a painful title. You know what it feels like?

It feels like shit.

Not long ago my husband told me I haven't been the same since my mother died. "You've lost your passion," he said. It was a rotten thing to hear—worse than "you've lost weight" when you haven't changed the number on the scale in years or "you look tired," on a day you're feeling particularly well. It was not a surface comment I could easily brush aside like a stray hair on a wool sweater. It cut deeply into what was left of my invaded spirit, especially because I understood what he meant.

My mother always knew me to be a passionate, spirited person. There

225

was rarely an in-between where my moods were concerned and Mom never failed to point out this fact. She often sent cards illustrating her opinion of my spirit: A little mop-headed girl throwing her arms open wide and a smile glistening toward the sky. Or a ballerina in a perfect, beautiful pose with a caption reading, "follow your dream wherever it leads." In tirades about war or the disappearing middle class, for example, or through discussions over hormone-injected dairy products and our need to grow organic vegetables, there was very little question where I stood. But ever since my mother died, these issues have lost their importance for me. As part of me died with her, my focus has shifted inward and remains more on my immediate family than on bigger issues I'll never fully understand. I still have opinions, of course, and go out of my way to see that my girls drink organic milk, but my passion for life issues outside my little realm has faded.

In my material life where I've lost seemingly important things like wallets, address books, and computer files, each has found an adequate substitute to serve its purpose and satisfy my need. With the loss of my mother, however, I can't find anything to replace the hole in my heart that opens each time I think to call and ask her a question, or share with her something my daughter said that reminded me so much of her. It's an odd, brief pang, and before my instinct to call her develops into a full thought that might lead to the physical movement of picking up the telephone, I push it aside. Silly me, I think. And it's over.

I guess we all find ways to cope with our losses. My dad, alone after fifty-six years of marriage, uses the phrase "Mommy left me" so often that it sounds more like a case of divorce rather than death. Some people talk out loud to their deceased loved-ones. It's been suggested to me more than once that I "talk to her" on the days I feel like calling. But speaking out loud in an empty room isn't something I do.

Knowing Mom was an avid reader of my weekly column, I sent copies to her each week. She kept the long, narrow clippings folded into accordions and tucked inside a small, flower-covered photo album. It was a brag book she filled not with pictures of the grandchildren I put off delivering, but the recorded meanderings of my life three thousand miles away from her nest. Each piece was lovingly filed according to date and they were interspersed with other feature articles I had written for various publications. I didn't know she had this album until just days after she died and my siblings and I combed through her lifetime of possessions, where we found piles of books filled with photos and clippings, and collections of papers keeping track of the lives of her five children. When one of my sisters found the brag book of my columns on display inside Mom's red secretary, she suggested I take it. But I didn't. I was happy to confiscate her 1940s Hummel of a little girl and a deer, (and I know two of my sisters have their eyes on that red secretary), but I didn't feel ready to take the brag book.

After my husband made the comment about my waning passion, however, I felt determined to somehow get it back. And so, as a first step, I asked my dad to send me the brag book. I was ready to review my past—to see my former self through a mother's eyes.

The exercise resulted in this book.

I confess that the above column, "Summer of Old," was not a part of her collection. (I found it on an old computer file.) I didn't have the courage to send it as I felt it would insult my mother, and even though aging and growing (and commenting on aging and growing) is an enormous part of a parent-child relationship, I would never knowingly or willfully insult her. In my current stage of the relationship where I play the role of parent, I make most of the comments. ("It doesn't look like you brushed your teeth;" "Comb that hair! You look like a ragamuffin;" "Do you really want to wear *those* pants with *that* shirt?") These types of comments are my entitlement as a mother and they fall out of my mouth like drool on a pillow. I'm parenting with my mouth open and I simply can't help it.

My children's comments on my appearance are limited; however, I count on them to rush toward me when I'm dressed to go out and tell me I "look pretty," just as my sister and I did on nights when White Shoulders perfume intoxicated our senses and we knew Mom was "gizzying" up. We watched her cascade down the front hallway stairs like a Hollywood movie star and crooned, "Ooh, Mommy, you're so beautiful."

Today my daughters have become my sister and me in the wafts of

The Things I Wish I'd Said

White Shoulders anticipation and while I relish their positive comments, I'm not sure how I'll feel when they start commenting on the deepening lines in my face or curly gray hairs spouting from my scalp.

I didn't notice my parents turning old until I moved to California. While they were always older than the other parents in the neighborhood, this didn't make them any less attractive or really any different from the other creatures stirring around in the alien world of grownups. But when I put together a collection of photos as part of my mother's eulogy, I saw her look changed gradually with the decades, just as it was supposed to. She evolved from a dark-haired, wide-faced beauty to a small, almost angular woman, who clearly preferred not to have her picture taken. She became the woman I picture in my head when I think of her today.

My mother was a tiny woman. Small by the standards of most, but tiny by mine. As I grew tall and shot past her while still in elementary school, I remember her quoting her height as five-foot-three and a half. That "and-a-half" was her little exclamation point. No one or nothing but age and osteoporosis could take away that half inch from her chart. I imagine she was five-foot nothing by the time she died. And according to our dad she weighed about eighty-five pounds.

She may have been small, but she had an enormous impact on my life.

She was eighty years old and she died doing what she loved: Water skiing. She didn't get up on her old, wooden ski on her last day, but gave it another valiant effort and suffered a stroke, a massive hemorrhage to the brain stem. With the help of his neighbors, who were out that morning taking coffee on their dock and looking forward to watching Mom's morning ski, Dad performed CPR until the ambulance arrived, and by helicopter, she was taken to St. Louis University Hospital and kept alive long enough for her children to arrive and kiss her goodbye.

The day after my mother died and I found myself in the sweltering July heat in the front yard of her home, I stood next to her favorite redbud tree. In the years just before her death my annual visits were always in April, which is when the redbuds in Missouri explode with small purple blossoms.

I have many photos of my daughters and their Nana taken in front of that purple tree. In July, however, its leaves were full and green and there were no signs of any buds, purple or red. In the furnace of the afternoon, I stared at the tree as if in a trance and wondered if the intense heat had caused my mother's stroke.

All at once a cardinal landed on a branch of the redbud and pierced the thick air with a shrill whistle. This bird snapped me to attention with its second, repetitive call, and then sucked me in like a worm as it sung a recognizable, rhythmic chirp. If you've spent any time in Illinois or Missouri as a child, you recognize the call of a cardinal the same way you know the sound of your mother calling you to dinner.

But I'll never forget that particular bird.

Although it was male, the cardinal in the redbud tree was just like my mother: It was beautiful, familiar and comforting, and it came when I needed it most. Behind its chirp I heard not only every cardinal that had ever sung for me before, but I also heard lyrics telling me that everything was going to be okay. I couldn't help but attach to this bird a spiritual message, which is repeated to me again and again by all the redbirds flying in and out of my life. And that message is: Life is beautiful and it flies by quickly. Remember not to lose sight of your passion.

It also sounded a little bit like my mother saying, "shit, shit, shit."

Conclusion

and

Acknowledgements

Wings, 1993

Not Previously Published

He's breaking out. Like a butterfly emerging from a thirty-year-old chrysalis, his legs kick and his wings form. He is finally growing up. And soon, if he makes it through this struggle, he will fly with a new self-confidence, a new stamina.

I watch him.

I observe with a hardhat and powerful pair of binoculars. I carry a shield. I carry a book. I listen to the deep breathing that comes with challenging work, to the heavy sighs, the cries, and even the laughter. I marvel at his progress and shake my head at his exasperations, quelling his desire to give up. I cheer him on like a pompon girl on the sidelines, ready to jump in reaction to any feat. More than anything, I want him to win.

And suddenly this game isn't easy. Someone switches the game plan at half time and forgets to hand him the rules. Or maybe the rules were handed out and he threw away his copy. After all, the first half had been easy. How was he to know that the blades on his shiny new skates were going to dull with age?

Once you find the easy way out, it doesn't make sense to look for a more complicated path. Your home is nice, your clothes are nice, and you have a lot of friends. Everyone seems to like you. And all the corners of Suburbia are soft. You have to look hard to find the craggy edges. But they're there, and you find them. You climb to the top of every hill without noticing the sweat forming on your young, handsome brow.

233

The Things I Wish I'd Said

You start to grow with an invincible attitude. You never question the gifts, accepting all that is handed to you as just part of the plan.

Nevertheless, it's hard to be the runt of the litter. At the tail end of a bunch of kids, the shadows of brilliant older brothers and successful older sisters loom large. Nicknames like "baby of the family" have a way of turning into "black sheep of the family," if you're not careful. So, if you care at all you have to try a little bit harder to get the recognition.

Examples are put before you and you are expected to follow footsteps that might not fit your feet. But you trudge along anyway to the applause of those who are only slightly paying attention. This applause encourages you—for a little while. And it's loud enough to help cover up the sound of that nagging inner voice that's suggesting to you "maybe this isn't the right thing for me."

"Who am I?" you ask yourself. "Who am *I*?"

You're not sure you really want to know the answer, so you keep climbing the hill, shrugging off comments from others that suggest you're not as invincible as you think. You don't hear them say that you might not have the lung power to keep ingesting all the black smoke that gathers 'round the top.

But then one day, something changes. Maybe it's as physical as a cough or a slap in the face. Maybe it's your first bounced check. Maybe you're left alone for the first time and you can no longer hear the applause or the warnings. Maybe that inner voice has started to scream.

"Damn it," it says. "I am *me*."

Dreams keep dumping him into his childhood home. He is always his father's son. He's feeling slightly mischievous and on the verge of being scolded again for something naughty he did yesterday, the day before, or just a minute ago when he buried his head in a soft feather pillow and said good night to his wife.

He wakes up in a cold sweat and reaches for the glass of water or the bottle of Tums sitting next to the bed. He's given up the other vices and this is what's left: A parched throat and an unsettled stomach. He is still too weak to emerge.

So, he settles back into the warm blankets, the king-sized cocoon, and closes his eyes. Just four more days until the weekend, he thinks. And then he falls back to sleep quickly.

I lay awake next to him, watching the fluttering movement of his long-lashed eyelids, and I imagine my dream for him.

I see him step outside his boyhood home and into a world filled with nothing but trees and flowers. He sees it and smells it all clearly for the first time.

He looks down at his fragile, wet wings and stretches them out like the stiff sleeves of a new shirt. He hesitates but then hears my soft whisper:

"Fly, my love, fly. I know that you can do it."

Wings Revisited

The above passage was written for my husband, Michael. Because of him, my life has soared to remarkable and exciting levels far past my expectations. He has gone beyond the call of both husband and daddy duty in helping take care of our beautiful children, Willow Gayle and Camille Ellen, and of course, in taking care of me. In the middle of this project, he even built me a new office because he grew tired of listening to complaints about being colossally disorganized in my hyphenated world. He also sat and listened to me read aloud each word and interjected and edited in his own funny and delightful way.

I must also thank my dear friend Debbie Hendryk, my Wilma, who came into my life at full bloom and continually makes me feel as though I'm the most fragrant flower on the shrub.

My other major influence is my sister and best friend, Gayle Van Lehman. Since we always comment about having had "the same life," I count on my Irish Twin to help fill in the blanks.

I lovingly acknowledge my parents, Tom and Kay, and thank them for all their support over the years, and to Mary Beth Urbanek, my sister and second mother, for your affection, sincerity, and frequent emails. No Ludite are you! Carl Schori, my reading buddy, you on the other hand, *are* a Ludite;

but I love you anyway and cherish our friendship and your frequent calls from a faulty cell phone.

Thank you to my friend Wendy Chestnut for saying I was funny, to my wise sister Debra VanOrt for too many reasons to list, but for now because her friend said I was funny. And thanks to my friends Bonnie Simmons and Anne Beaver for actually being funny.

To my friends at St. Alban's, thank you for your spiritual support and guidance.

Thank you to Chip and Mary Brown, former publishers of *The Montclarion* newspaper, now owned by the *Contra Costa Times,* and to my editors, Nancy Kieffer and Don Hill.

Thank you to Mary Beth Rosenthal, owner of Morning Star Traders and Antiques in Tucson, for your portrait and your friendship. Thanks to Chelsea Hendryk and Camille Cozzens for your portraits, too. Thanks to Jeanine Ertel, Carol Craig and Salleé Gerbing for your consistent, loving support, and to Julie Widman, Jane Curatola, Karen Schwarz and Susan Davey for your wisdom and kindness. Thanks to Barbara Kingsolver for your inspiration and encouragement. To Eric Bollinger, Jr. at McKenna Publishing Group, thank you for your help and patience, and also to Leslie Parker for your design expertise.

Finally, many thanks go to Ric Bollinger of McKenna Publishing Group, who turned me from a writer to an author and made the process worthwhile. Your professionalism and sense of humor are truly appreciated.